Waterside
A Pictorial Past
CALSHOT – FAWLEY – HYTHE – MARCHWOOD

Waterside

A Pictorial Past

CALSHOT – FAWLEY – HYTHE – MARCHWOOD

Clare and Fred Murley

Ensign
PUBLICATIONS

First published in 1991
by Ensign Publications
a division of Hampshire Books Ltd
2 Redcar Street
Southampton SO1 5LL

Reprinted 1992

British Library Cataloguing in Publication Data
 Waterside a pictorial past: Calshot – Fawley – Hythe – Marchwood.
 1. Hampshire. South-west Hampshire. Social life, history
 I. Title II. Murley, Clare and Murley, Fred
 942.275

ISBN 1 85455 068 3

Edited by David Graves
Typeset by PageMerger
Printed by Bell & Bain, Glasgow

Preface

We came to the Waterside in 1951, the year the Fawley Oil Refinery went 'on stream' and was formally opened by Clement Attlee. Our first pharmacy in a tiny shop in Fawley Village was only justified by the great influx of people that the industry brought to the area. As it continued to grow, so did our business and our commitment to many interests and activities in village life. A talk to the Fawley Community Association in 1959 on 'Old Fawley' brought an enthusiastic response and the Fawley Local History Group was formed. My wife Clare became deeply involved and has led the collection of photographs, memories, and records of the life of the parish ever since.

The group has since been renamed Fawley Historians and the collections are now substantial. We have drawn on them for this book which is but a small sample of the wealth of material available. Our purpose is to stimulate more interest in recording the rapidly changing story of the Waterside parishes.

Our sincere thanks are due to the members of Fawley Historians for their help and encouragement, their patient work in collecting the material and their support to us both over many years.

For myself, photography has been a continuing interest from schooldays, a substantial part of our business and the means of adding many unique moments of the present and the past to our collections. In the course of this I have learnt a great deal. My aims are now to analyse and catalogue, but primarily to institute modern methods of conservation of the photographs, the copy negatives and the written material – an expensive task for a small group of enthusiasts. A large part of the proceeds from the sale of this book will be devoted to this purpose.

Since we retired to live in Hythe we have been able to draw on the assistance of members of Hythe Historians and our thanks are also due to them and to all those who have helped us greatly over the last thirty years by teaching us what to do, by donating or lending for copying their precious photographs and documents, and by writing or talking to our members and allowing us to record their memories of times past.

Fred Murley
January 1991
Hythe

Foreword

The 'Waterside' is a modern name. The title now binds together the parishes that line the western and usually sheltered side of the Southampton Water. In years gone by, the hamlets were well separated. John Wise in his *New Forest*, published in 1862, observed of the stretch south of Hythe that:

> True English lanes will lead us by quiet dells, with glimpses here and there through hedge-row elms of the blue Southampton Water down to the shores of the Solent.

Wise in his wanderings saw only the odd mansion, collections of cottages and small fields. A few years before his book was published, smugglers had provided colour, while fishermen, longshoremen and those engaged in agriculture made up the majority of the workforce. On the great manors, blacksmiths, brick-makers, brewers, bargees, gardeners, grooms and keepers were highly skilled.

Ferrymen plied from Hythe to Southampton and from Lepe to Gurnard on the Isle of Wight. Preventative men kept watch and pilots vied for jobs. There were few shopkeepers, more publicans and a carrier. The doctor, the parson and the squire had their places, but publicly-funded education had to wait 'til Wise's time and later to be available to all. There were 'poor houses' for the needy. There was one at Fawley, later a cottage, demolished after the last war. The villages had a hum about them and a neighbourliness that has had the edge turned by the growth of the population and the increasing pace of life.

The great change started in 1912 with the establishment of the sea-plane base at Calshot, later the venue for the Schneider Trophy races. The AGWI refinery came in 1926 and Esso in 1947. The Waterside though had quietly absorbed events before of national and international importance without much change of scenery. Cerdic the Saxon had literally altered the face of Britain when he landed in Stanswood Bay in AD495 and Marconi changed our habits when he perfected his wireless from Luttrell's tower by Eaglehurst before the First War.

Fred and Clare Murley have long devoted themselves to highlighting the past and to telling this story, illustrating these changes through the lens of the famed local photographer Edward Mudge. They have gathered together a remarkable record of all the happenings, particularly since the Waterside 'woke up' in 1912.

Maldwin Drummond, OBE, JP, DL
May 1991
Cadland House

Contents

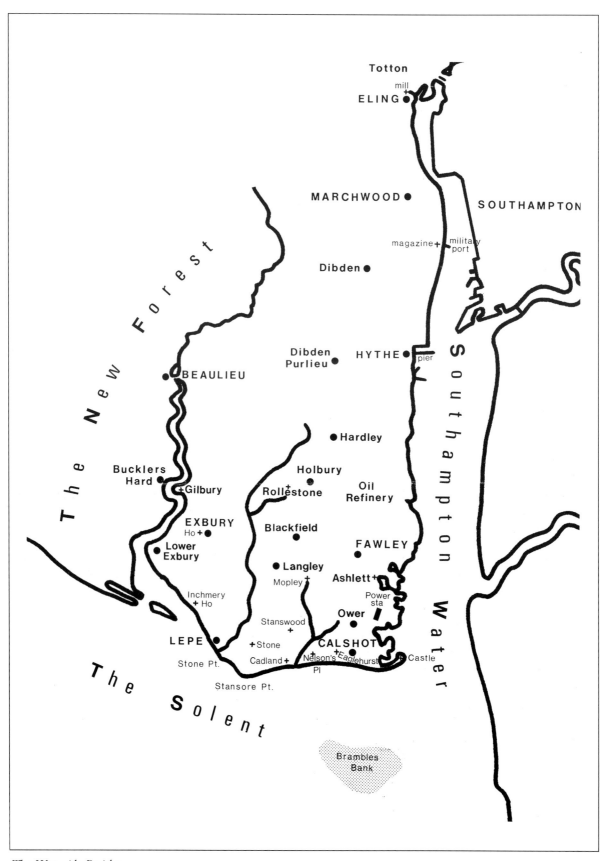

The Waterside Parishes.

Introduction

"Why the Waterside?", asked our publisher. It seems to us well-named, a natural tag for the parishes of Eling, Dibden, Hythe, Fawley and Exbury. They are all at the water's edge and together are a strip of land squeezed between the ancient boundary of The New Forest and Southampton Water, about ten miles in length from Eling to Calshot, but hardly anywhere more than two miles wide between Forest and shoreline. Never clearly defined by manorial, ecclesiastical, or political boundaries, we continued, yet it is quite a separate and distinct region.

There are few evidences of prehistoric peoples. We know that Romans were here but if they lived in a villa or a fort, it has yet to be discovered. Its history perhaps begins in 495 AD when the Anglo Saxon Chronicle records that Cerdic the Saxon and his son Cynric with five ships landed at 'Cerdices-Ora' and on the same day, defeated the natives. Calshot, in its early forms of Calshore, Caushot or Caulshore, with its sheltered landing place of Ower Lake, may well have been 'Cerdices-Ora' but as the lake site is now covered by Fawley power station we shall probably never know for certain.

Since early days the land was little changed, small villages or hamlets, scattered farms, with fishing, forestry and husbandry the only occupations. A paternalistic Estate employed and sheltered many. All this has changed completely in just two lifetimes. The Waterside is now a place of industry and commerce and a major dormitory suburb of Southampton.

For as long as the New Forest survives however, the Waterside cannot expand beyond its present limits, so it is not just a geographical location but a very pleasant place in which to live. Watersiders are only a few minutes away from heathland and shady woods, or from the open water and pleasant beaches.

"Very well", said our publisher, "A history of the Waterside it shall be".

As the most westerly parts of the Waterside, Lepe and Exbury are the best preserved, we start our look at its history there, on the banks of the Beaulieu River. Then moving along the Solent shore to Calshot before turning north to look at Fawley, Hythe, Dibden, Marchwood and the approaches to Eling. Bartley Water or perhaps the Test must mark the northern boundary of the Waterside area, conveniently separating us from our larger neighbours.

Ower landing before reclamation.

Beaulieu River 1854 – A water colour.

Chapter One

The Solent Shore

Exbury

The marshy coastal fringes of the Solent and Southampton Water, like those further east in Hampshire, are rich in the variety of birdlife to be seen; Geese, Duck and waders of all kinds. In 1904 when Edward Mudge came from his family home, hard by the West Gate, Southampton, to live in Fawley he already knew this area well. The year before he had recorded in his diary a day afloat,

> ...in due course Beaulieu river was reached when after breakfast, somewhat hurried, I continued on until above Gins. Years ago the farmer there, after neglecting his business, saw it sold piecemeal, until he had to take to the river to provide himself and his family with a living. This he did I was told by fishing in the Summer and shooting with the big gun in the Winter.

For several years he himself went wild-fowling along these shorelines and made his living, shooting for the markets in Southampton and London. His keen observation of the wildlife around him was essential for success, "...in outwitting and surprising some of the wily birds..."

He found photography useful to record each 'bag' and this hobby gradually became his main business. He had a natural talent for describing these scenes and an eye for a picture through his camera lens. Very many of the photographs that he took in the next fifty years and more, were to be of the Waterside, its villages and their people. They are a valuable record of his time and a wonderful source for the historian.

For many years he kept his punt by the old brickyard at Lower Exbury on the banks of the Beaulieu River. The bricks made here from local clay were very light in colour and were used for many of the houses in Exbury village and its surroundings.

Lower Exbury is the site of the original village, a small fishing hamlet where boats could be pulled up on the beach. Before 1827, services were held in an ancient chapel at Lower Exbury itself which in days gone by was served by the Cistercians from Beaulieu Abbey, the tradition being that the monks crossed the river from St Leonards on stepping stones. The earliest mention of a chapel was in 1291 when

> Master Nicholas de Audeby held the church of Fawley with the chapel of Exbury.

The Manor of Exbury is a large estate of fertile ground with farms and woodlands bordering the Beaulieu River and its estuary. It was purchased in 1718 by William Mitford who lived in Gilbury House and his grandson, another William, created the present village. Here in 1827 a church was built, the old chapel at Lower Exbury was pulled down and the stones dispersed, some being used to build a folly in the garden of the house while others became part of local pigsties. It remained a chapelry of Fawley until 1863 when the Curate in charge became Rector.

In 1892 gradual modernisation of the Church began with new oil lamps to light it, for services had previously only been held in daylight hours. By 1907 extensive repairs to the roof were necessary so it was decided to take the opportunity of lengthening the whole building and replacing the ugly slate roof with the present tiles. The flat ceiling gave place to vaulting which added greatly to the height. The new external facing of Ventnor stone required additional

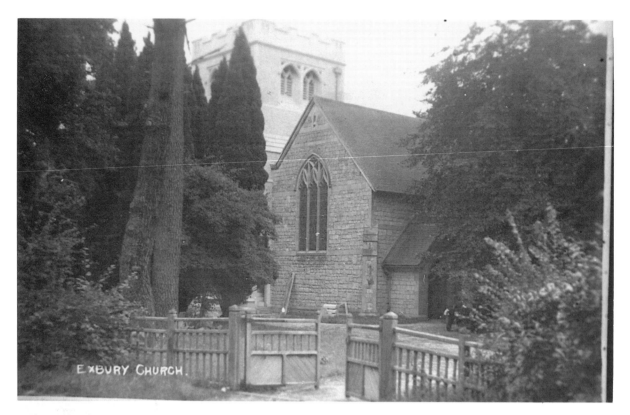

Exbury Church.

Exbury village – 1900s.

foundations, and these incorporated the original stones from the ancient chapel, retrieved from the folly and the pigsties, thus once more forming part of a sacred building.

The Mitfords had sold their Exbury lands to Major John Forster in 1879. His son Harry inherited the Manor and married Rachel, daughter of Henry, first Lord Montagu of Beaulieu. Harry Forster was an accomplished athlete, playing cricket for Hampshire in 1895 and had a distinguished political career. He was created Baron Forster of Lepe in 1918. Tragically, both their sons died in the Great War of 1914/18 and a memorial chapel now forms the base of the tower which the Forsters added to Exbury church in thanksgiving for the allied victory. It contains a bronze sculpture of the younger son by Cecil Thomas R.A. which was exhibited at the Royal Academy in 1924 and was the original from which others were cast for war memorials in other parts of the country.

Lord Forster became Governor General of Australia at this time and sold the main part of the estate to Lionel de Rothschild, a member of the international banking family who already owned Inchmery House nearby. He had been a great friend of Lord Montagu since his early twenties and a frequent visitor to Beaulieu. Between them they developed fast racing boats with Napier engines and raced at Cannes in 1907, winning the Perla de Mediterraneo and breaking the world record speed of 28.8 knots. Mr Lionel moved to Exbury in 1919 and immediately began to enlarge what had been William Mitford's original house in a classical style, refacing the brick with stone but taking care to preserve a magnificent magnolia against one of the side walls.

One of Mr Lionel's great interests was horticulture and he specialised in Rhododendrons, Azaleas and Orchids. At Exbury then, there was only The Glade with tall cedars and a giant Redwood tree, the rest of the 220 acres being an English woodland garden. A workforce of some 200 men cleared the undergrowth from the many mature trees, laid out 10 miles of paths and as Rhododendrons are water-hungry plants, 22 miles of pipe were fed with water from a bore hole via a water tower.

When war came in 1939 changes were inevitable. Mr Lionel de Rothschild died in 1942 and the house, with others near Exbury and Beaulieu, were requisitioned by the Admiralty as a shore establishment, *H.M.S. Mastodon*. His son, Edmund, had very little time to store the contents of the house or protect the interior before sailing with his regiment to North Africa.

Mastodon became a headquarters, where plans were prepared for the D-Day landings. The Hon. Mrs Pleydell-Bouverie remembers that the Allied Chiefs of Staff came to Exbury House for debriefing afterwards.

When the war ended the house became two training establishments, *H.M.S. King Alfred* and *H.M.S. Hawk.* Inchmery House where the S.O.E. (Special Operations Executive) had been installed for the final training of undercover agents before they made contact with the resistance forces across the channel, was de-requisitioned first but it was not until 1955 that Exbury house itself was released, together with the many nissen huts which surrounded it.

After his war-time service, Mr Eddy, as Edmund de Rothschild is affectionately known, began to restore its gardens and fulfill his father's plans for Exbury. His personal aims are to allow the public to share in the glories of these magnificent gardens,

Exbury House.

while placing them on a sound business footing and retaining the skills necessary to develop further varieties. Some of the largest trees were casualties of the storms of 1987 and 1989 but this has opened up new vistas and created a changing scene.

From Exbury to Eaglehurst

If we look at this stretch of beautiful coastline from the sea – to the west, Exbury House and Inchmery are glimpsed among the trees and Lepe House stands out at the mouth of the Beaulieu River. Eastwards is a line of cottages above Lepe Beach and then a wooded shore with Cadland House the only prominent feature until we see Luttrell's Tower above the trees, before the long low line of Calshot Spit, where its castle at the extreme end guards the entrance to Southampton Water.

Before the great storm of November 1703, it would have seemed very different. A large part of the Brambles Bank was then swept away and vast quantities of shingle altered the whole of this shoreline dramatically. Lepe harbour was damaged, that of Stoney Point destroyed and the old harbour of Ourd on the Bourne stream vanished as shingle closed the

entrance. The histories of these places and of the houses facing the water are inextricably bound up with the lives of their inhabitants – fishermen and landowners, shipbuilders and farmers, smugglers and revenue men.

Lepe was a good little fishing port, the Darkwater stream which had a mill on it, flowed through the valley and came out alongside the cliff where the car park is now. According to ancient tradition there was once a ford here across to the Isle of Wight, whether this was so or not, the sea passage from Gurnard to Lepe was certainly a favoured route up to the first Elizabeth's time. There have been various spellings of the name over the years – Leope, Lupe, Leape and Leap have all been used. Traces of a Roman road or trackway leading from Lepe can be found going inland through King's Rew, Langley and Butts Ash past the tumuli on the heath towards Nursling and Southampton with a branch westwards to Ringwood.

Those lost harbours had made use of sheltered natural creeks running deep into the coastline. Poor roads ashore made transport difficult so it was much easier to move goods by sea from place to place. The harbours of Stoney Point and Ourd no longer appear on a chart of 1786 and a nearby settlement around

Lepe House – 1913.

Stone Farm has also gone. The mouth of the stream at Bourne Gap was closed by the shingle bank which quickly became stable and in the 1840s after a gully and sluice were put in, the reclaimed land was used for growing barley. Travelling from Lepe to Calshot today the road dips sharply to the valley bottom at Little Stanswood Farm where there was once a mill. From here the stream is now a drainage ditch through a nature reserve down towards the shore at Bourne Gap. After the old harbour silted up a sedge 'Island' formed in the mill-pond and Scots Pine trees grew there. In the 1911 Kelly's Directory it records

> ...until about 1866 there was this land of about three acres called 'The Floating Island' with trees from 25 to 30 feet high upon it and which at certain seasons moved to and fro, but by the draining of the surrounding mass has become fixed.

At Lepe the process of silting was much slower and a period of shipbuilding took place. In 1744 the Navy Board were seeking sites near the Royal Dockyards. Lepe was surveyed, a favourable report made and Moody Janverin, a shipbuilder at Hamble, took the opportunity to create a new yard here. The gravel beach with the low cliff behind it provided a site for him to build the *Greenwich*, 1053 tons, launched in April 1748; followed by the *Fowey* of 513 tons in July 1749. Henry Adams who was building 7 ships for the Admiralty at nearby Buckler's Hard, found that his newest commission, the *Europe*, a 64 gun ship of 1370 tons, was too big for that site so it was built on the stony shore at Lepe. The launch was accomplished with some difficulty on April 21, 1765 and with this Lepe's shipbuilding days were ended.

At the western end of Lepe beach on the cliff, in a commanding position at the entrance of the Beaulieu River, stands Lepe House the core of which was formerly the *Ship Inn*, an alehouse as early as 1752 where shipwrights and caulkers were paid their wages.

A map of 1825 shows no remaining harbours for by this time Lepe had also silted up and gone out of use – only Brickyard Quay at Lower Exbury was still busy. Soon after this we can draw on personal memories to learn more about Lepe and the Solent shores. First, F.J.Penny, writing to *The Hampshire Advertiser* in 1927 about the three vanished Inns of Fawley, said

> The Ship at Lepe, formed the nucleus of what is now known as Lepe House and I can readily visualise the old Inn sign over the side door of the well-frequented house (still but little altered in itself though of course much added to) when I stayed there in 1857 for several days. The highly respected landlord was then dear old James Wheller, of whom the mortal part has long since reposed in the graveyard of Fawley Wesleyan Chapel. Mr Wheller's landlord was Mr Percy Mitford of the noble house of Redesdale. The Lepe estate was sold to Major Forster and the old Ship Inn thereupon ceased to be.

Major John Forster's son Harry succeeded him and lived here in Lepe House, becoming Lord Forster of Lepe.

Next, George Bowyer, born in 1859 and like Edward Mudge from just by Southampton's West Gate. His father and uncles were pilots of the port, as he recounts in his book *Lively Ahoy – Reminiscences of 58 Years in the Pilotage Service*. At the age of twelve he left school and joined his uncle in the pilot cutter *Lively*. Lepe was the western end of the pilotage station for Southampton,

> At Lepe we had a pair of moorings well inshore; and what is now Lord Forster's house greatly enlarged, was a public house kept by a Mr Rowe and he was very friendly with the pilots. Being a boy, I used to like going ashore with them and having a good run around....Winkles in those days were very plentiful along Lepe mud to Lymington, and a couple of hands with a bucket could fill it in a very short time during the season....There were several noted old characters about Lepe. One was an old coastguard pensioner and he lived in an old fishing boat turned bottom up on the beach, it made quite a snug little home, with a little window or two, plenty of tar outside and was quite weatherproof....I believe his name was Dunn....In those days at Exbury there was a good trade in bricks (straw coloured)....Lord de la Warr, living nearby at Inchmery had moorings just inside the river for his fine large barque-rigged yacht, the *Edeline*...

Thirdly, Thomas Soffe, born in 1899 recalled his early life growing up in his home at Stone Farm which was part of the Manor of Stone mentioned in Domesday and which had been farmed by his grandfather,

THE STATION. LEPE.

Watch House and Coastguard cottages, Lepe

Back in the early days harvesting was done with the scythe. Richard Graveney would get a gang together to mow a field for a given price. They would work from dawn to dark, but first thing Richard would do is bring two gallon jars of beer from the Ship Inn at Lepe – the landlord was Joe Rowe – and the men would have two pints to start the day. Tom Langford and his brother Bill had a barge to take about 10 tons; they traded to Newport on the Island and to Southampton, bringing coal to the Brickyard Quay at Lower Exbury...

Mr Soffe remembered it being bought from the barge and bagged for home use at Stone Farm,

...Barley from the Fawley area was much sought after by the brewers as they liked the taste it gave the beer. It was loaded on to the barge at Brickyard Quay or at low water near Stone Point and shipped to four breweries, Mew Langtons at Newport, Scrases at Southampton, Asbeys at Totton and another. It came from local farms, Stone, Stanswood, and perhaps Whitefield's. The barge brought back fertiliser and oil cake from Dickson and Carter at Eling Wharf...

This was all remembered from the years before the 1914/18 war when a load of grain from Exbury to Southampton by barge cost one shilling (5p) per ton.

Twenty-two years later the Solent shores were at war again and this time they were in the forefront of enemy attacks. In 1944 preparations for the allied invasion of Europe sealed off this coastline for ten miles inland, closing it to all visitors. Local residents, farmers and agricultural workers found their movements severely restricted and they became liable to spot checks. A few remnants of the structures for embarking the D-Day forces can be seen along the beaches and a ramp of concrete 'Biscuits' still leads down from the road at the western end to the river in front of Lepe House, but personal details of the time are scarce. A large work-force moved into a camp above the present car park and work began on highly secret projects. Thomas Soffe again recalls,

When contractors were building the bottom halves of the concrete caissons (for the Mulberry harbour) at Stone Point, I had to sign the Secrets Act. I delivered milk daily to the canteen there. A railway line ran from the Point towards Bourne Hill Cottage and the caissons were built like cars, rolling off the assembly line into the sea where they were pulled by tug to Southampton dry dock for the top section to be cast...

Each of these Phoenix caissons was almost as big as a five storey block of flats, 200 feet long, 55 feet wide and 60 feet high, and each weighed 6000 tons.

Perhaps the best picture of Exbury and Lepe at this time is found in fiction, but written with so much descriptive detail and local knowledge that the Southampton author, Neville Shute, must have known the area well. In his novel *Requiem for a Wren* he describes it in March 1944,

> ...activity increased in the Beaulieu area, and with it came mysteries. Lepe House, the mansion at the entrance to the river, was taken over by the Navy and became full of very secretive naval officers; it became known that this was part of a mysterious naval entity called Force J. Near Lepe House and at the very mouth of the river a construction gang began work in full strength to make a hard, sloping concrete platform running down into the water where the flat-bottomed landing craft could beach to refuel and let their ramps down to embark the vehicles or tanks. This place was about two miles from Mastodon. A mile or so along the coast a country house was occupied by a naval party who did strange things with tugs and wires and winches and with what looked like a gigantic reel of cotton floating in the sea; this was Pluto, Pipe Line Under The Ocean, which was to lay pipes from England to France to carry petrol to supply the armies which were due to land in Normandy. On a bare beach nearby a thousand navvies were camped making huge concrete structures known as Phoenix, one of many such sites all along the coast...

In the late build-up to Operation Overlord the narrow country roads to Lepe were widened and passing places made under cover of the trees. Late in May 1944 the woods around were packed with troops and the roads crammed with tanks, guns, ambulances and army vehicles of all kinds. On 6 June, the great armada sailed and after a while Lepe was quiet again.

Beyond Lepe to the east is the present Cadland House, replacing the Drummond family mansion which formerly stood on the site of today's Esso refinery at Fawley. It grew out of the fishing cottage at Bourne Hill, built in 1780 when the original Cadland House was being constructed at Fawley,

The Drummond Family – 1781.

Bournehill Cottage – 1913.

European Magazine.

EAGLEHURST, HAMPSHIRE,
The Property of the Earl of Cavan

Engraved by Rawle, from an original Drawing by I.Nixon Esq.

Eaglehurst.

both were designed by Henry Holland. Zoffany's painting, a delightful conversation piece, showing Robert Drummond and his family at Bourne Hill may have been painted just after this time.

Lancelot (Capability) Brown laid out a landscape garden to complement the cottage itself which was a double octagon, one being the drawing room, the other containing a kitchen and an extra room. A stair led to three rooms under the thatch, but the building's life was short indeed, for on Thursday July 7 1785, Robert Drummond was entertaining a party of gentlemen in the cottage and they were "merry" after lunch when, "...about 3 o'clock smoke was observed to issue from the building, and in less than an hour it was consumed". The furniture was, "...happily saved..." by all the gentlemen, except Robert Drummond, who was "...soon missed...". With "...the most provident calmness of philosophy...", he had been rescuing wine from the cellar and "...giving directions for a splendid service of refreshment". As it was a sunny afternoon in July, Robert and his guests were able to sit down and enjoy "...a fine haunch of venison...and some excellent wine" – presumably on the lawn, with the smouldering cottage on one side, the Solent on the other and the main house three miles away.

The cottage was rebuilt on the same foundations in 1786. In place of the inflammable thatch, Henry Holland gave it a slate roof and a balcony. Rowlandson, the artist and caricaturist (1756-1827) sketched the house when he toured the New Forest and Solent shores at about that time. Holland also designed two 'little' wings in 1803 and the cottage was obviously well-loved and used. It was enlarged from 1865 onward, when Lady Elizabeth Drummond moved there from Cadland, her son Edgar succeeding to the estate. Holland's cottage was finally destroyed by fire in 1916 and the new house was built on the site in 1934. During the last war the front of the house was protected by a stockade of Scots pine posts and a high bank of earth. This shielded the house from shrapnel from the two bombs which fell close-by in the sea. It was restored to use by the Drummond family and renamed Cadland in 1948. A restoration of Capability Brown's garden began in 1983, using the original plan held in the archives with the architect's drawings, bills and correspondence.

George Bowyer, the pilot, also recorded,

> ...In bad weather, often with winds from the S.W. to the N.W., we would go up into Stansore Bay and find more shelter, anchoring off Lady Elizabeth Cottage; and just to the N.E. was Eaglehurst belonging to Squire Drummond, but let for many years to a Count Batthyany. The Count (a member of the Royal Yacht Squadron) owned a fine large racing cutter of about 120 tons, named the Kreimhilda and a very nice little steam yacht named the Blunderbuss which was admired by everybody.

Eaglehurst, or Luttrell's Tower is a conspicuous landmark rising 110 feet above the trees from its 30 feet high Eagle Cliff, with superb views of the Solent from Portsmouth to the Needles to seaward, while towards the land is a panorama of the New Forest and Southampton Water. It was built in the mid 1700s by Temple Simon Luttrell, son of the Earl of Carhampton, a member of a colourful if slightly disreputable Irish family. It has cellars beneath and a tunnel, (now closed) running to the beach was perhaps older than the tower itself judging by a scratched date of 1731.

Luttrell died in France in 1803, his folly having been sold to his brother-in-law the Earl of Cavan who was a General and second-in-command to Sir Ralph Abercrombie during the Peninsular Wars. On his return to this country the Earl took up residence in the tower, but even with his tents around, it was too small for his needs, so he decided to build a house on the landward side. It was designed to remind the General of his campaigns, being in the form of his encampment with his own large tent in the centre, flanked with those for lower ranking officers on either side. This impression was reinforced by the interior, for the ceilings of the rooms simulated the curves of the canvas.

In 1830 there were disturbances throughout the country. Widespread Land Enclosures had deprived many of the agricultural workers of their own plots of land and wages were pitifully low. A reporter from *The Times* said that in this area the movements of hungry men could be traced by turnip parings along the roadsides. During the protests which became known as the Swing Riots, men gathered at Eagle-

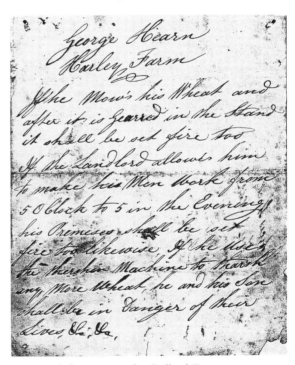

Poster nailed to a tree in the Cadland Estate.
George Hearn
Harley Farm
If he mows his wheat and after it is gathered in the stand it shall be set fire to.
If the landlord allowes him to make his men work from 5 o'clock to 5 in the evening his primeses shall be set fire to likewise.
If he uses the thershin machine to tharsh any more wheat he and his son shall be in danger of their lives, ha! ha!

hurst and threatened to hang the Earl unless something was done to help them. The riots were quelled and wages were increased to some extent.

The young Princess Victoria visited Eaglehurst in 1833 and recorded in her diary,

> Lord Cavan, Lady Lydia his daughter and Lady Cavan had arrived there before us in order to meet us. It is a very singular place; there is a very high tower near the sea, but they live entirely on the ground floor like tents. There is not a staircase in the house. It is very comfortably furnished and quite like a cottage.

When the Earl died, Eaglehurst passed to his grandson who decided to sell it in 1843. At this time Victoria, now Queen and married to Prince Albert, visited it again when they were considering the purchase of a marine residence. The local unrest created by the Swing riots may have been one of the reasons why Osborne on the Isle of Wight was chosen instead.

To prevent Eaglehurst being converted into a seaside resort, Andrew Robert Drummond bought it and the estate leased it, first to other members of the Drummond family, then to a succession of people, among them Count Batthyany. In 1906 it was let to Guglielmo Marconi who had a laboratory in the top room of the tower. He was able to transmit signals to his yacht *Electra*, moored in Cowes Roads. In 1912 he and his family were invited by the White Star Line as their guests on the maiden voyage of the *Titanic*. Fortunately Marconi left three days earlier on another ship and the rest of the family were delayed by his son Giulio's sudden illness. Degna, his daughter recalls how she and her mother climbed the tower on the morning of April 10th to watch the *Titanic* sail by. Degna was hardly four years old, but she remembered vividly,

> ...together we waved at the ship, huge and resplendent in the spring sunlight, and dozens of handkerchiefs and scarves were waved back at us. As the Titanic passed from our view over the calm water we slowly descended the steps. It was a long way down....

The tragedy of the sinking of the 'unsinkable' liner had thus nearly destroyed the family, but Marconi's genius did save many lives subsequently.

In the last war, the Royal Air Force and the Royal Navy took over the lease, steel shutters covered the windows of the tower and the cottages were used for billets. The buildings were much damaged so that after the war when it was bought by Colonel Valder Gates of 'Cow and Gate' fame, he had to restore it extensively. In recent years it passed to the Landmark Trust who sold the house but retained the tower in an effort to preserve it for posterity.

Inland from Eaglehurst, on the road to Lepe, was a small hamlet with a pub, the *White Horse*. Lord Nelson is said to have landed on the beach one day and called in for refreshment. After enjoying his drink he asked

> "What is the name of this place, landlord?"

On being told 'Lazy Town' and yet observing many people apparently busily employed about their tasks, he reputedly banged his glass on the bench, saying,

> "A very stupid one. I name this – Nelson's place!."

F.J.Penny (*Hampshire Advertiser* of 1927) remembers,

> ...the attraction of the merry (wild cherry) gardens added to that of good ale vended amid peaceful rural surroundings, drew much custom to the White Horse, numerous wherries coming across from Cowes with people, whilst the villagers also were constant visitors to the secluded and orderly old Inn....

The Inn is no more but the cottages behind *Nelson's Lodge* on the roadside are still known as *Nelson's Place*

Smugglers and Preventive Men

Since the time of King John duty has been payable on imported goods and customs men have been employed to collect the dues as well as to prevent evasion by smugglers. In time of war, Preventive Officers added to these duties those of preventing the coming and going of passengers, the passing of intelligence and the transmission of correspondence. By the beginning of the 1700s a peace-time force of Riding Officers guarding the south coast was established to prevent the movement inland of smuggled goods that had evaded revenue ships at sea and the customs officers in the ports. The Riding Officers eventually formed the nucleus of the coastguard service, but it wasn't until early this century that the Board of Customs and Excise was established.

The shoreline hereabouts, like so much of the south coast, had small inlets, tidal creeks and shingle beaches, all good landing places and often with wooded banks giving cover for the fishermen and wildfowlers; ideal spots to conceal illegal activities. For some three hundred years country folk and seafarers have used their knowledge of the shore and hinterland to smuggle contraband. Locals still tell many tales handed down in their families, embroidered no doubt and losing nothing in the telling. By 1820 hundreds of items had been added to the list of taxed goods and smuggling was rife. The luggers of these 'Free Traders' were now fast, well manned, armed and often able to resist a challenge from the customs' vessels.

William Arnold (father of Dr Thomas Arnold, head of Rugby school) became Collector of Customs at Cowes in 1778. He was an outstanding man of great ability and integrity when others in the service often received rewards for information or for 'turning a blind eye'. For some years he complained that he could see the passing traffic of the smuggling fraternity in the Solent from his post ashore, but alas, no revenue cutters were stationed in the vicinity to deal with them.

From 1815 a waterguard supplemented the Preventive Officers and the cutters *Repulse* and *Lion* were stationed near Calshot Castle. After this there were many affrays off the coast and seizures of cargoes at Lepe. Billy Coombes, captain of a smuggling boat was betrayed and captured when his ship was disabled; he was hanged from a gibbet at Stoney Point, by Lepe Beach.

It may be that the reason Simon Luttrell built his tower in such a commanding position was its value as a watch-tower and signalling point in his smuggling activities. He was believed to go personally to France to select brandy for his wealthy customers in high places and this may well have been a reason for his arrest there and imprisonment in 1793.

On one occasion a betrayal took place and a signal was sent indicating the absence of Riding Officers by one of them who had noticed great activity at the tower from his look-out position at Calshot Castle. The remains of a previous cargo were found with men waiting for the next. When this arrived they were surprised by customs men lying in wait and were seized together with their cargo.

The hamlet of Spratt's Down behind Eaglehurst was dubbed 'Lazy Town' because the men were said to sleep during the day. Agricultural work was very poorly paid, but they could earn five shillings (a week's wages) for a night's labour shifting contraband. Once cleared from the beach and the tunnel at Eaglehurst, caves at Spratt's Down and Mopley were used as storage until it could be moved on by cart or pack-horse.

The Coastguard Service proper was formed in 1831 and after Trafalgar some Royal Navy ships were freed from other duties and were able to assist the Revenue Service. A coastguard station was built at Lepe and the Watch House on the beach with its solid foundations, has withstood many buffetings from rough weather since then. It has a long-ranging view of the Solent from Cowes in the east to Hurst and beyond in the west. The cutter was kept below the house and although this is now in private occupation part of the slipway can still be seen. The row of coastguard cottages on the cliff above the beach were stoutly built of local brick in 1857-60. The men manning the station were listed in the 1841 census as a Commander, who was a Royal Navy Lieutenant, with two servants, two commissioned bo'suns, one mounted guard and four coastguards, all on regular pay. With this stable employment they became a part of village life and of the church at Exbury.

Eaglehurst, Luttrell's tower and Top Camp – 1960.

Chapter Two

Calshot and Eaglehurst Camp

When Henry VIII succeeded to the throne of England in 1509 on the death of his father Henry VII, almost his first act was to marry his brother Arthur's widow, Catherine of Aragon. At this time Europe was dominated by France, Spain and the Holy Roman Empire, with the balance of power between them continually shifting as one alliance succeeded another. As King of a country less powerful than any one of these and an ambitious man, Henry involved England in European politics and military campaigns, expanded the Navy and for some years kept his enemies at bay, by shifting his allegiance from one nation to another. He was concerned that he had no male heir and resolved to divorce Catherine; this led to the break with Rome, the establishment of the Church of England and the dissolution of the monasteries. In 1538 the Emperor Charles V and Francis I of France signed a ten-year truce and planned an invasion of England to re-establish the Pope's authority.

Action to defend the country was quickly taken, the fleet was assembled, the chain of beacons repaired and manned and special commissioners appointed to "search and defend the coastline".

In a short time, a series of forts, batteries and blockhouses were planned along the Channel coast facing France, from Sandown, Deal and Walmer in the east to Pendennis and St Mawes in the west. It formed a major part of the whole defence system from Hull to Milford Haven.

The Solent, Southampton and the Isle of Wight were considered particularly vulnerable and the commissioners appointed for this area were William Fitzwilliam, the Lord Admiral and Earl of Southampton, with William Paulet, Lord St John. Earl William in a letter of March 1539 to Chancellor Thomas Cromwell was concerned with, "..the building of a tower at Calshotes Poynt".

Construction at Calshot was largely finished by the end of 1540, probably some stone from Beaulieu

Calshot Castle.

Abbey was used, certainly we know that lead from there was taken for its roof as Henry had signed a warrant to this effect in the previous year. Although Calshot was one of the smaller forts in the defence plan, it was a good strategic position, situated at the end of a long shingle spit and on the brink of the deep water channel at the entrance to Southampton Water. It commanded then, as it does today, an extensive view of the approaches and all shipping entering and leaving the port.

The castle itself was built as a three storey tower or keep surrounded by a curtain wall and moat. Over this, a wooden drawbridge gave access to the narrow bailey. The level of water in the moat was controlled by a sluice gate through which it entered from the sea at high tide. Stairs to each of the floors and the roof were made in the thickness of the wall. It was one of the most heavily armed of the Solent forts, with a total of 36 heavy guns designed to fire through the gun-ports in the tower and curtain wall as well as embrasures on the roof.

John Leland recorded in the 1540s that, "...at the west point of it (Southampton) is a stronge castelle late builded caullid Couldshore, communely Cowshot".

It is believed that the guns were never fired in anger but the test of these defences came in July 1545 when Francis I attacked Portsmouth with 225 ships and 30,000 men. Henry, forewarned, was in Portsmouth as Commander-in-Chief of the Army and Navy. Land defences were prepared, the beacons were lit and the English fleet made ready in the harbour. The French had meanwhile anchored in St Helen's Roads off the Isle of Wight. There was an inconclusive skirmish, but the next day the King's ship, the *Mary Rose* sank when going about and the sea rushed in through her open gun-ports. The French withdrew although raiding parties landed in the Island at Brading, Bonchurch and Sandown to burn houses and take some lives before being repulsed by the local militia.

During the next two centuries, the castle's history is uneventful and little is recorded, but we do know from a pay list that in Elizabeth's reign there was a captain at one shilling a day, a subaltern at eightpence, four soldiers at sixpence, a porter at eightpence and eight gunners at sixpence each. The Queen ordered the "..mountynge of ordinance..", when Philip of Spain was expected to sail up "the narrow seas" in 1567.

The Spanish war of Elizabeth's reign brought about an increase in privateering. The prize jurisdiction was of importance to Southampton and the

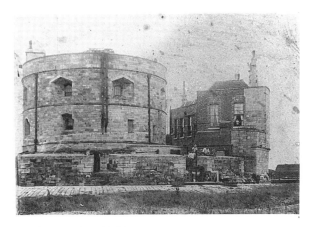

Calshot Castle – 1900.

Calshot Castle – The gunners.

town records contain much of interest about this period.

In 1572 a Captain James Parkinson was Governor of both Calshot and Southampton castles. He and his garrison used Calshot to waylay ships and extort dues in the form of part of their cargo before allowing them to pass, rather than protecting them from piratical attacks which were a constant hazard even in home waters.

His men were imprisoned in Southampton after committing various misdemeanours in the town and there was a confrontation between Parkinson and the mayor, who by his office was (Southampton's mayor still is) Admiral of the port. Parkinson threatened to crack the mayor's crown, but words only were exchanged and the mayor then took depositions from those who had knowledge of what was happening at Calshot.

John Solton, a baker, told of seeing packs of Spanish wool, spices and sugar arriving by night. One of the stables at Calshot was packed full of such wool and he expressed his disgust with the language and behaviour of the soldiers.

A Breton pilot told how Parkinson's men caused his ship, *Marge of Bennenden* to remain off Calshot for ten days, each day removing half a butt of 'sack'. Many such complaints were made and when in Parkinson's absence the men began to take two butts from passing ships, he was forced to order them to, ".. take but one – and see that it be full!"

The situation does not seem to have been resolved, ships were still shot at and the goods taken were sold in Southampton, but of Parkinson's end we know nothing.

Calshot Castle had been deteriorating during this time and although surveyed in James I's reign, nothing was done until the Civil War, when a Royalist demonstration in Southampton was answered by a Parliamentary gunboat which damaged Calshot, and destroyed Netley and St Andrew's castles on the opposite shore. The town hastily assured Cromwell of its fidelity to Parliament, reparations were made and a full repair of the fabric of the castle at Calshot took place, so that in 1648 it was declared to be, "A place of great strength".

Little seems to have disturbed its peace thereafter and in 1695 that intrepid lady, Celia Fiennes, who travelled widely through England describing it in her journal noted,

> ....about 3 leagues off is Cashot Castle just out into the sea, which does encompass it all but a very little point of land called Horsy Beach that runs out into the New Forrest by Bewly which was an Abby in the Forrest, for the extent of the Forrest is large miles long; all round Cashott Castle on the Beach on the beach itts as full of fine Cockle shells so they heap them up all round the Castle like a wall;.....

The Spit was often breached at high tide isolating the castle, until the great storm of 1703 swept vast amounts of shingle along the coast and made the Spit a permanent feature. The castle was still manned during the 1700s and the registers of Fawley parish record the burials of men and their families who served in it.

Alterations to the fabric to strengthen it when required for defence were made over the succeeding years, but at quiet times only a caretaker garrison was stationed there. After the Napoleonic Wars the castle was used as quarters for the coastguard and in the 1851 census William Mitchell, James McNiell, James Fletcher, and Edward Maylen were listed as such, with their families; together with Thomas Hodgson, Master Gunner, Royal Artillery and his wife Maria. The revenue cutter was moored safely in the shelter of the spit, but ready at all times to pursue and contend with smugglers in the Solent or Southampton Water.

The Admiralty took over control of the Coastguard Service in 1856 and the castle passed into their hands. In the late 1860s when the Whitehead torpedo was being developed, navies began to experiment successfully with torpedo boats. In 1886 the Admiralty considered taking down the upper part of the tower, filling in the moat and surrounding what was left by earthworks in order to create a torpedo station to protect the approaches to Southampton from seabourne attack by foreign torpedo boats. However, this idea was dropped and it was decided instead to install QF (quick firing) guns and searchlights on the outer forts to destroy these craft if such an attack was launched.

When the Admiralty handed the control of Calshot to the War Office, large scale additions, alterations, the re-arming of the castle and of the spit itself were put in hand. A battery of six QF guns was built where the hangar which houses the Activities Centre now stands. Three of the gun embrasures in the curtain wall were adapted for searchlights to be installed and generators powered by oil engines were put in the basement of the tower. A boom across the entrance to Southampton Water was added to these new defences to protect it from attack by surface craft. It was a cumbersome system however and was replaced in 1909 by a lighter structure which could be stored on the slipway next to the castle, it stayed as an effective defence until the end of the 1914-1918 war. At this period too the last of a series of replacements of the old quarters within the castle took place, the roof was strengthened to take an extra pair of 12 pdr QF guns, while its garrison was increased in a 1910 mobilisation plan to three officers and 85 other ranks.

The Advent of Aircraft and the First World War

In April 1912 the Royal Flying Corps was formed to be followed later that year by the Royal Naval Air Service; the Admiralty decided to set up a chain of air stations from Scapa Flow to Pembroke Dock for the defence of the coastal waters of Britain. The Calshot Royal Naval Air Station came into being on March 29th 1913 with Lieutenant Spenser Grey R.N., as its first Commander. He was living at Southsea and travelled to Calshot and back daily in his own private seaplane.

Calshot R.N.A.S. Wintertime 1914-1918.

The Calshot Express.

Living huts at Top Camp.

Until war was declared the flying was largely experimental, testing various types of float plane for possible use by the naval wing of the R.F.C.; Winston Churchill, as First Lord of the Admiralty actively encouraged naval aviation and had his first seaplane flight from Calshot on August 28th, 1913. That same year the station assumed responsi-

bility for Area Customs, Coastal Intelligence and Meteorology.

Squadron Commander A.M. Longmore (later Air Marshal Sir Arthur Longmore) took over the command of No.1 Squadron R.N.A.S. from Spenser Grey in January 1914; apart from the flying itself, the techniques of gunnery, torpedo work and submarine detection were studied. The latter was only found possible in calm water conditions and was demonstrated to Winston Churchill, in February, 1919. Longmore flew to Portsmouth in a Maurice Farman to collect Churchill and take him over a submarine submerging at varying depths. Longmore himself had made the first successful torpedo drop from a seaplane on July 28th, just six days before war was declared on the 4th August, 1914.

After these early trials and experiments came training in earnest, but these were formative days in the history of flight and war in the air. The memories of Wing Cmdr Sir John Hodsell tell us something of Calshot at this time,

> As a young Flight Sub-Lieutenant I was posted to the Royal Naval Seaplane base at Calshot. I had just ten hours flying time to my credit on Graham White 'Box Kites' and Maurice & Henry Farmans at the Graham White School at Hendon. The Admiralty had posted me there in October 1914 on my first commission. Calshot then was bounded by mud flats, saltings, and creeks – the haunt of wildfowl, and at sunset it was a make-believe land of subtle tints and colours.
> Beside Calshot Castle were perched sheds to house seaplanes, a tin hut (formerly the Castle Yacht Club) to act as the Officers Mess, and coastguard cottages used as cabins, duck boards made walking on the shingle more tolerable. It was as compact a little station as could be wanted. The castle had come to life again, sentries paced its ramparts and guns of the Territorial Army Coastal Battery prepared to repel invaders who might escape the vigorous attention of the Spithead forts. Occasionally they would fire blanks when recognition signals appeared unsatisfactory. Here young pilots and mechanics had the dual task of training others to fly seaplanes and flying boats, and to scour the Channel for enemy submarines. Our craft were a motley collection – the Sopwith seaplane which had won the Schneider Trophy in 1914, a Sopwith Bat Boat (an amphibian) with a 120 HP Austro-Daimler water-cooled engine, two Nieuport monoplanes fitted with floats, a B.E. from Farnborough, a Sopwith tractor christened 'The Honeymoon Bus', F.B.A. flying boats, and a dockyard tug *The Controller* to tow them home again when the engine stopped or they hit the sea rather harder than was good for them.
> For attacking submarines our earliest weapon was a bomb carried in the lap which was tossed over the side. Later it was suspended in a canvas sleeve held by a split pin lashed to the pilot. Finally a high explosive bomb appeared with a proper, if primitive bomb rack, a toggle release for the pilot and a simple but effective bomb sight. Serious patrolling was done in Short Seaplanes fitted with a 225 HP Sunbeam engine which thought nothing of shedding its propeller, and on one occasion a whole cylinder block which embedded itself in the starboard float.
> To get into many of these machines it was necessary to be carried out on the back of a wader – sometimes with the inevitable result. It was a great day when flying boats of a respectable size arrived from America..."

Before the end of the war, the QF guns were removed and the area taken into the Station which was now expanding rapidly. The contractors were Henry Boot and Son Ltd. and they laid down a light

Schneider Trophy 1927 – R.J. Mitchell's Supermarine S5.

Supermarine Southampton flying boat.

railway line along the Spit from fields near Eaglehurst, where an accommodation camp was also being built, with a spur to a gravel pit nearby so that materials could be transported easily to the sites at the 'Top Camp' as well as at the seaward end of the Spit.

In April 1918 The R.N.A.S. and the R.F.C. were amalgamated to become the third service, the Royal Air Force and at Calshot No.1 Sqdn. R.N.A.S. was renamed No.201 Squadron R.A.F.

The Years between the Wars

The Station now became the School of Naval Co-operation and Aerial Navigation and in 1922 it was renamed Royal Air Force Base, Calshot; made up of Headquarters Flight, No.480 (Coastal Reconnaissance) Flight, The Seaplane Training Unit, the Air Pilotage Flight, and the Marine Craft Training Section. This latter part of the Station's duties expanded gradually over the next four years and in 1927 it became the principal R.A.F. centre for teaching marine engine fitting and marine craft maintenance in addition to motor boat crew training.

New aircraft began to arrive at Calshot to replace the old Felixstowe F3 and F5 flying boats. The most successful were the Supermarine Southamptons, one of R.J. Mitchell's flying boat designs for that company, supplied with wooden hulls in 1925. A duralumin hulled version followed and as the Mark II, stayed in service until 1936, with a crew of five in separate cockpits, a wingspan of 75 feet and powered by two Napier Lion Va (500 HP) engines. In 1927 the Far East Flight of four of these planes made a completely successful 27,000 mile tour of duty to Australia and Hong Kong via Singapore.

The Schneider Trophy

Great Britain had won the 1914 contest at Monaco with a Sopwith Seaplane flown by Howard Picton at 86.8 mph. The first post-war race at Bournemouth was declared void because of fog and there were no British entries at Venice in 1920 and 1921. At Naples in the following year, an R.J. Mitchell designed Supermarine Sea Lion II flown by their pilot Henri Biard, won a very close race at 145.7 mph. At Cowes in 1923 however, the Sea Lion III was beaten by the American Curtis C.R.3 and in the next (1925) contest at Baltimore, Mitchell's radically new design, the Supermarine S4, crashed the day before the race.

By this time it was realised that competing for the Schneider Trophy was too costly for individual, or works teams. The R.A.F. now undertook to select and train a group of specialised pilots and the High Speed Flight as it was known, made its home base at Calshot. There was no British entry in the 1926 race at Hampton Roads, U.S.A. which was won by Italy.

Meanwhile the foremost aircraft firms and engine manufacturers in this country had been developing new designs with government support and six machines were ready for the 1927 contest at Venice. Two of these were Mitchell's Supermarine S5s, three were Gloster IVBs, a bi-plane design, both using Napier Lion VIIB engines and the Short Crusader with a Bristol Mercury, air-cooled radial engine. This plane crashed on test, the Gloster retired, but Flt. Lt. Webster won in an S5 at a speed of 281.65 mph. Development of new planes for the next race began, but tragedy struck in March 1928 when the High Speed Flight returned to Calshot to make an attempt on the world airspeed record. Flt. Lt. Kinkhead was killed when his S5 crashed into the sea and he was buried in Fawley churchyard among the graves of other R.A.F. men. In the September, Flt. Lt. D'Arcy Greig set a new British air speed record of 319.57 mph, just short of a world record.

For the 1929 contest at Calshot, Mitchell designed the S6 to accommodate a Rolls-Royce 'R' engine, and this was to be matched against the Gloster VI Golden Arrow, an American entry and three Macchi seaplanes from Italy.

Calshot, and beaches along the Solent to Southsea and on the Island were crowded with more than a million spectators, many of whom had camped there

R.A.F. High Speed Flight. L to R: Flight Lieutenants, H.M. Schofield, O.E. Worsley, S.N. Webster, S.M. Kinkead, and Squadron Leader L.S. Slatter.

Calshot beach, September 7th 1929.

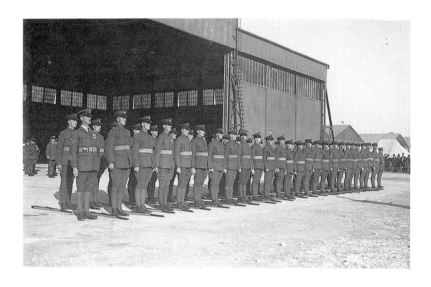

R.A.F. parade at Calshot.

Empire Air Day souvenir 1934, with Fairey F4 seaplane.

overnight and cooked breakfast in the early morning. It was said that the fragrance of eggs and bacon spread for miles!

The American entry and the Gloster were withdrawn before the race itself, which was won by F/O Waghorn in the S6 at 328.6 mph, the Macchi M52R coming second at 284.2 mph. On September 12th, Sqdn. Ldr. Orlebar piloted Waghorn's machine over a 3 kilometre straight-line course at 357.7 mph, a new world record.

However, to retain the Schneider Trophy itself, Britain had now to win for the third consecutive time in 1931. Preparations were hampered by the threatened withdrawal of Government support in the face of the great depression of 1930. It seemed that an attempt might not be possible until a private donation of £100,000 by Lady Houston made it feasible. Since only nine months remained in which to develop a new machine and train pilots these were testing times for the industry. Rolls-Royce increased the power of the 'R' engine and at Supermarine Mitchell decided to modify the S6 to take it and the increased fuel which had to be carried.

The High Speed Flight had been joined by Lt. Gerry Brinton, R.N. F/O R.A.F. of the Fleet Air Arm, but in an accident off Calshot during training he was killed when the S6 which had won the last contest crashed. The Italians too had their tragedies when the two Macchi MC72s crashed, killing their pilots.

So it was that there was no other competitor and Flight Lieutenant Boothman had only to fly the new S6b over the course safely on the 13th September 1931, to win the Trophy outright. This he did averaging 340.08 mph over the seven laps. Two weeks later with the same machine and a still further modified engine, Flt. Lt. Stainforth set a new world air speed record of 407.5 mph.

Among the many R.A.F. personnel involved had been Wing Cmdr S.W. Smith from the Mount Batten Station at Plymouth, he brought with him as his personal assistant Aircraftman Shaw who had been concerned with the testing of fast marine craft for the R.A.F. Shaw was of course better known as T.E. Lawrence, or 'Lawrence of Arabia'.

The High Speed Flight was disbanded, it had served its purpose, the lessons learned and Mitchell's designs which culminated in the Spitfire, had a profound and lasting effect on the aircraft of World War II, but before that, Calshot's faithful 'Southamptons' were replaced in 1936 by Saro 'Londons' built by Saunders Roe at Cowes. Other flying boats that also

Saro Cloud amphibian flying boat.

appeared at Calshot were, Saro 'Clouds', Supermarine 'Scapas', 'Walruses', 'Stranraers', 'Singapores' and 'Rangoons'. The first 'Sunderlands' came in 1938 to replace nearly all the others as the most versatile of the Second World War's marine aircraft.

There were other aspects of aviation development and the history of the R.A.F. in which Calshot played a part in the twenties and thirties. At nearby Hythe, Hubert Scott-Paine was building fast boats to capture the world water speed record and from his early high speed launches (HSLs) came generations of small boats to service and support the aircraft. They were tested, accepted and then ferried by Calshot crews to R.A.F. bases all over the world. Some of the later and larger versions saved many airmen's lives in the Second World War as fast Air Sea Rescue boats.

The Schneider Trophy contest itself was only a small part of the work of R.A.F. Calshot during those years between the wars when hundreds of men were trained here to carry out many tasks in aircraft and marine craft handling, armament, servicing and repair. We can sample something of this varied work as well as the life-style of its men and women by drawing on their memories, first of peace time in 1936 to 1939.

Aircraft

It is hard for anyone not on Flying Boats to realise the different attitude you have to adopt on being posted to them. It is a world of its own completely under the influence of the weather and the sea. Spit and Polish goes by the board when salt spray covers everything.
A.F.D.

Aircrew

The crew of the flying boats, in addition to the pilots, consisted of a fitter and the wireless operator. The fitter looked after the engines, which he had to start manually on the Southamptons by means of a starting handle. The wireless operator had to be up in the bows ready to cast off from the mooring buoy as soon as the second engine started, also he had to moor up the boat to the buoy at the end of flying. The fitters of course much later became flight engineers on the newer flying boats such as the Stranraers and Sunderlands.
P.W.

The Railway

Calshot's Light Steam Railway was known affectionately to many for forty years as *The Calshot Express*. Its construction work done, it stayed on until 1947 to ferry passengers and transport stores between the Spit and the Top, or Eaglehurst Camp.

The officers and senior N.C.O.'s rode to and from the bottom camp, on the Spit by the light railway. The train used to leave Eaglehurst camp, about a mile north-west of the castle where the living quarters were, about 7.50 a.m., but we airmen had to walk!
We marched along the Spit to the hangers in column of fours with the station band at the head to make marching easier.
P.W.

One of its 0-4-0 locomotives, an Andrew Barclay Class E well tank was renamed *'Douglas'* and is still working on the Talyllyn Railway.

Duties

The duties of our crews were standby safety launches, Crew ferrying to Aircraft, Torpedo running and recovery at Stokes Bay and Flare Path night duties for bumps and circuits training for the Southampton Flying Boats.
J.C.

I spent a very happy eighteen months at R.A.F. Calshot. At that time I was a photographer. The photographic section was a small corrugated iron building near the coastguard cottages. A new section for us and the armourers was then in course of construction near the large hangar.
S.E.C.

Pay

We were paid a shilling a day extra for every day on which we flew, which on a basic pay of 5 shillings per day was appreciable.
P.W.

Eaglehurst, or the Top Camp

I have many happy memories of Calshot...It consisted mainly of accommodation, NAAFI, married quarters, gym, a small church and a central parade square...it was an old camp with buildings that were very primitive by today's standards. Each man had a bedside locker and a wall (lockable) one, a steel lattice bed with three 'biscuits' as a mattress. There were no springs at all in the bed. Blankets were issued and sheets and pillow cases changed every week. The huts had a toilet and four wash hand basins at one end which were kept clean every day by a room orderly...the baths and showers were in another hut and were available for all. You had to keep your bed space polished and cleaned every day, and a special tidy up once a week ready for an Officer's Inspection. In addition, each was allocated a job by the Corporal in charge, cleaning fire buckets, coal bins, lamps, windows. There were two coal bins, one at each end and every week there was an issue of coal, to be collected in them. They were of steel, but kept highly polished and looked a picture against a blacked stove and a highly polished floor.

These jobs were taken as normal and never considered a chore. Once a month we had a general parade and hut inspection...however primitive the huts may have been, they were kept in a state of excellent cleanliness.

Reveille was 06.30, Men were on parade at 08.00, and lights out was at 22.15. The Church (St George's) was small, so only a proportion of each section was detailed for Church Parade on Sunday.

We worked a normal week, with a half day on Saturday, and Sunday off unless detailed for duty.   A.F.D.

Recreation

On the camp itself there were the usual sports, rugby, football, etc. The principal feature was the camp boxing team. Matches were held in the gym and outsiders invited in...it was also used twice a week as a cinema, open to people from the married quarters and outside the camp as well. Being a flying boat base, there were facilities for the men to have water-born sports. For the officers there were 12 and 14 foot International Dinghies, while for the men there was a 27 foot ex-naval whaler.   A.F.D.

The Second World War

1940 – Five seaplane tenders left Calshot for the beaches of Dunkirk, two were sunk on the first run-in, the other three rescued nearly 500 men.

> I remember so well marching in the winter morning darkness along the Spit from our sleeping quarters to the cook-house. Never did breakfast taste so good.   E.A.

> In the main Calshot was a pilot training and maintenance base. In the early days (it) was No. 2 Training Squadron. As well as maintenance crews to keep the aircraft flying there was a Marine Craft Section which involved High Speed launches, Seaplane Tenders, refuelling vessels, bomb practice vessels, pinnaces, and dinghies. Within months hundreds of airmen passed through Calshot having been trained as seamen to crew the various vessels before being posted to other flying boat coastal command stations such as Mount Batten (Plymouth), Pembroke Dock, Stranraer, Lerwick etc.
> A.B.C.

> I can remember standing by Calshot Castle and watching Cowes being bombed and of course every time we visited Southampton, a little more of it had disappeared.   G.P.

Seaplane tender ashore, winter 1940.

1944 D-Day

Cycling down to work, we suddenly give a start as we look out to sea. For the first time in days you can actually see the water again. Yesterday there were thousands and thousands of ships, rows upon rows of them, all shapes and sizes. And this morning there is just plain, clear water, green waves breaking mockingly on the pebbly shore. Someone says it means nothing. Just an exercise. But nobody believes her. We cycle on in silence. And the date is June the Sixth.   E.M. (WAAF)

Fourteen Air Sea Rescue HSLs were sent from Calshot to the beaches to give additional anti-aircraft fire and to recover airmen who had to bale out.

Some of us were made up into crews for the HSL's, we went to Dover, then back to Poole and Calshot from where we covered the D-day landings. We sailed very early in the morning to make contact with a radar L.C.T...We were told to follow it...but our engines were too powerful, even on one alone, so we asked to be towed, but this pulled them off course so we had to let go. Sometime afterwards we lost contact with this vessel and heard later that it had been sunk.

We were there to cover the airborne landings, the invasion ships passed all around us. We used to do four days at the beachhead and four at Calshot...it took us four hours to get across from Calshot.   R.W.

The Post-War Years

In 1948, Calshot and its 'Sunderland' flying boats played a great part in 'Operation Plane Fare' as the Berlin air lift was known, more than a thousand sorties were flown to lakes in the city carrying vital supplies in and ferrying out refugees. When this was over, the squadrons were transferred back to Pembroke Dock and flying virtually ceased at Calshot.

The coastguards returned to the buildings which had been added to the top of the castle and the Southampton Harbour Board leased its roof for a large radar installation. The R.A.F. presence, (238 Maintenance Unit) still worked at the repair and upkeep of all types of marine craft until in April 1961, R.A.F. Calshot finally closed its gates.

Before that, Calshot had become the last resting place of two of the three largest flying boats built in this country, the Saunders Roe 'Princess', intended to carry 200 passengers in the post-war period. Powered by ten Bristol Proteus engines, 140 tons in

Airmen on Marine Fitters Conversion Course.

Sunderlands off R.A.F. Calshot.

weight and 148 feet long, only one was completed and actually flew, the other two were cocooned and stored here for a while until finally broken up.

A sad end to Calshot's part in the story of flight from the first fragile, float planes of the start of the century, to R.J. Mitchell's sleek S6b. From only a few miles an hour to over 407 in less than 40 years.

Eaglehurst Camp became a temporary home in 1961 for the population of Tristan da Cunha who were evacuated when the volcano on their island erupted. Many of them returned later when it was safe to do so but some stayed on to make a permanent home in the little street of houses that were built as married quarters and later became war-time billets for the WAAFs. It is now Tristan Close and together with St George's Church and the former Officers Mess, are all that remain of 'Eaglehurst', or the 'Top Camp'. The mess is now *The Flying Boat Inn* but for a while used the squadron badge of the *Owl & Crescent* for its name.

The coastguard presence is now just a tall tower.

The buildings on the Spit have found other uses, a lot of experimental work was done there in the sixties to perfect 'Dracones', large flexible tubes used to transport fresh water or light fluids in the sea. Towed behind a tug, they were easily rolled up when empty for the return journey. The project is still under development in Scotland.

Calshot's hangars now train another generation of young sailors and athletes in many different sports and pastimes. A very appropriate use for these vast covered spaces, so long devoted to training and the passing on of skills, service, and tradition. The castle has been shorn of its radar scanner and the old flight control and meteorological buildings. Its ownership has been transferred to English Heritage who have restored it as nearly as possible to its appearance just after the turn of the century.

We can once more climb the narrow stair in the thickness of the wall to come out onto its roof and look over the parapets at the same marvellous panorama that Henry VIII would have seen 450 years ago.

Chapter Three

Fawley Village and Ashlett Creek

From Calshot northwards to Fawley is still a country road until we reach the entrance to the Power Station, where it becomes much wider and by-passes Fawley village itself; very different from John Wise's description of the way from Hythe to Calshot in 1883 as "..true English lanes which lead us by quiet dells, with glimpses here and there through hedgerow elms of the blue Southampton Water" Not so long ago many of those trees still lined the Calshot road and the lanes on either side, making them into shady green tunnels, until Dutch Elm disease came in the mid-seventies, made wholesale felling necessary and created today's wide open views of the water.

Before 1925 the roads in almost the whole of the Waterside were of gravel, uneven and full of pot-holes, dusty in Summer and muddy in Winter. In that year a petition was organised to protest at their poor state and unsuitability for heavier traffic, resulting in the principal stretches being tar-macadamed before long.

Before that time, many of the goods and supplies needed by country people were transported by the

local carrier. In 1843 John Arnold of Woodington (near Mopley) and Richard Willis of Ower (near Calshot) served the Fawley and Calshot areas. In 1849 we know that Richard travelled to Southampton every Tuesday and Saturday, returning from 118, High Street at 3 pm. Richard's daughter Harriet aged 17, married 22 year old William South at Fawley in 1862 and they then ran the business, being joined by their son Jesse, whose son, another William, also became part of 'South's the Carriers' – relied on throughout the Waterside right up to the 1960's, more than a century of family service to the community.

In 1912 their horse-drawn wagon was succeeded by motor omnibuses and Mr South's *Forest Queen* and *Gypsy Queen* were popular with R.A.F. personnel from Calshot Air Station as well as local people. In opposition for some while was George Wheeler of Fawley whose horse-drawn coach, nicknamed *The Fawley Flyer* carried passengers and parcels to Southampton on Mondays, Wednesdays and Fridays for 6d. single or 9d. return, the equivalent of less than 5p in decimal money.

The coach itself has survived and has been restored by a group of local businessmen. It was inspected by the Queen and Prince Philip at a gathering of the Commoners and their animals, with the British Driving Society, on Whitefield Moor in 1979, the 900th anniversary of the founding of the New Forest.

It took a long time to establish a regular public transport system for the whole of the Waterside. There was an early attempt to bring a railway line from Beaulieu Road Station which had been opened in 1880 and was well used for goods and livestock as well as passengers, but this failed in the face of opposition from landowners. So in 1906 The Lon-

The restored Fawley Flyer in Fawley, 1979.

L.S.W.R. Thornycroft bus at Blackfield cross roads.

Single-decker bus at Ower (Calshot).

don and South-Western Railway introduced a Thornycroft motor bus which ran four times daily in Summer and twice daily in Winter from Totton Station to Blackfield and Fawley. It travelled at about 12 m.p.h., amid complaints of its unreliability until 1910.

From 1929 the Hants and Dorset Bus Company ran a regular service from Southampton to Calshot and known, more or less affectionately, by the R.A.F. as 'The Pants and Corsets'. They fought off competition in 1932 from the Premier Motor Service who tried to take their customers by starting off from Calshot a few minutes earlier, eventually they absorbed that company and maintained the principal connecting link for the whole Waterside until recent years.

The South family did not compete with the bus service, but started a taxi business and also continued the regular collection and delivery service to and from Southampton three times a week. William South's regular trip was timed such that he left the *Dolphin* yard in the High Street at 2.00 pm. When in the early days of our business at Fawley, we needed something urgently, we could ring a Southampton wholesaler, ask them to take the item to the *Dolphin*

Hotel before two o'clock, knowing that we would be sure to have it for our customer later that afternoon for a very small charge.

Before going to Fawley, turn off to the right and go down the narrow lane called Stonehills to Ashlett Creek. From much earlier than the times we have been talking about, Southampton Water had been the obvious alternative to those gravel roads and coastal barge traffic was already an important part of the life of the villages. Bulk supplies of coal, coke and oil were brought into Ashlett Creek from Portsmouth, Southampton and the Isle of Wight in sailing barges with names like *Bessie*, *Vixen* and *Ackton*. The *Vixen*, owned by William Major of Fawley Square later broke her back in the creek and ended her days in the mud near Calshot. In his account books we find an item:

> ...For the hire of a boat from Southampton to Fawley with 15 tons of coal and same delivered at Calshot Castle in December 1907 at four shillings per ton...

In the following years, the *Ada*, *Empress*, and *Mary Emily* regularly transported stores, soil, manure,

A barge at Ashlett Quay before 1920.

grain, and timber in and out of the creek. One lady recalled that as children, she and her brother played in the marshes at Ashlett near her grandmother's house. They picked up spilt pieces of coal into buckets; and for sixpence they could go to Southampton and back on the barge belonging to old Mr. Martin, the landlord of *The Jolly Sailor* when he went to collect his supplies of beer. Another lady, daughter of Mr. Giles the grocer in Fawley, remembered how they used to go to Swanwick in the same way for Strawberry picking.

The barges were designed for easy handling by a small crew, usually two men, or perhaps two men and a boy, but the hardest part of their job was loading and unloading. They had a weekly wage, no matter how long they worked, but the more tonnage they carried the more they earned. Working the tides in a creek like Ashlett which dries out at low water was critical. If, for instance on a Neap tide, they were able to get away in the early morning and with a fair wind make Newport at the head of navigation in the Medina river, off-load during the day, and return by the evening, the tide would still serve to let them enter the creek. They could then re-load, and take the barge out to anchor off the creek ready for the next day.

About this time the Williams family bought the barge *Exchange* and were trading in the area. Their present firm is still the Williams Shipping Company (Fawley) Limited, of Southampton although they no longer use the creek. The last big sailing barge to come into Ashlett was *The Britisher*, brought in by Mr.C. Tillyer in 1932.

One barge still remains at Ashlett Creek. The *Medina* was used at the end of her sailing life, as a lighter by the contractors Christian Nielsen at the building of the present Esso jetty. When she was accidentally holed she was beached and stripped and her remains can still be seen in the mud at low water. When the road system was improved and the need for barge traffic declined, Ashlett lost its commercial importance, is now the home of the Esso Sailing Club and private yachts occupy the moorings.

Ashlett Mill at the head of the Creek was powered by the tides. A date stone is still visible high up on the face of the building which reads 1816, but there may have been a mill on this site for far longer than that. A tidal mill was regularly rated from 1660 to 1680, while a document records that Eva de Clinton, widow of a Norman knight, bequeathed "Cadland Mill and all its appurtenances" to the Abbots and Cannons of St Mary, Tichfield in the 14th Century. After the mill ceased working in 1910 it became a store and part of it was used by Mr Theo Smith, the boat builder, to assemble an early aeroplane, probably *Moonbeam I* for the Southampton aviator Eric Rowland Moon, a hole in the wall had to be made to get the wings out and local people remembered seeing it being taken to Webster's field but no one now recalls seeing it in flight.

After the first World War, A.G.W.I. (The Anglo, Gulf, West Indies Petroleum Corporation) had permission from the Board of Trade to build a small refinery on Southampton Water. They purchased a portion of land and salt marsh adjoining Ashlett Creek from the Drummond Estate. Construction began in August 1920, initially bringing many tons of shingle from Langstone by barges into Ashlett as land-fill and to make a road access to the site by widening and surfacing Marsh Lane from Fawley church down to the shore. As we have seen, the roads at that time were unable to take heavy traffic and the proposals to link the site by rail with Beaulieu Road or Lyndhurst Road Stations were considered again, but discarded because of the need to avoid encroaching upon the New Forest.

The Totton, Hythe and Fawley Light Railway Company was formed and work on the line was begun, but the project was not completed in time to assist in the construction work. Instead, the Victoria Quay at Ashlett opposite the mill was repaired by the Fawley Parish Council and the creek became a small port for the refinery. A narrow-gauge railway ran from the quay alongside the mill pond into the construction site and eventually became quite an elaborate system serving the whole refinery. A standard gauge steam crane unloaded steel plates from Belgium for the oil storage tanks, pipe work for the plant, and concrete piles for the jetty, in fact most of the materials needed for the refinery came into Ashlett by barge and were handled in this way.

Ashlett Mill served as a hostel for the workers who came from some distance. The labourers were organised in gangs to move the large amounts of earth by hand shovelling it into horse-drawn side-tipping trucks to prepare the ground for the storage tanks, the buildings and the plant. The first load of crude oil came ashore and was discharged into tanks in June 1921. Sir Joseph Davies, Chairman of the company reported at the first Annual General Meeting that "..on the 11th August 1921, in exactly one year we had on our Director's table a tin of petrol made at our own refinery from crude oil imported at our own wharf. I think that you will agree that this is a remarkable record of quick work..."

The Jolly Sailor in Mr Martin's time.

The Totton, Hythe and Fawley Light Railway part of the enterprise was handed over to the London & South-Western Railway which became part of the Southern Railway in 1923, so the problem of a Waterside railway link was resolved and the first passenger train steamed into the new Fawley Station in Marsh Lane on July 20th 1925. In its early days it was crowded with workers to and from that first A.G.W.I. refinery at Fawley, besides the Power Boat Company and B.O.A.C. at Hythe, such that seats were difficult to find at busy periods. It was said that the line was never run with passengers in mind, apart from the workmen and as its role of carrying goods and materials in, as well as the products of the refinery out, increased, so did its passenger traffic decline. The last passenger train ran in 1966 and the Station site is now within the Refinery itself, but the line continues to carry large amounts of petroleum products away from Fawley.

The *Jolly Sailor*, Ashlett's cosy, welcoming pub has refreshed sailors and visitors for many generations with the energy needed to climb the winding hill to Fawley.

The village of Fawley itself originally centred around All Saints Church, the Falegia or Falalie of Domesday. A diocesan document mentions the owning of church land in 971 AD. A small aisleless building of Saxon foundation was extended and cha-pels added by the twelfth century. Among the church plate belonging to All Saints is a 14th century silver patten given by William of Wykeham, Bishop of Winchester and also an Elizabethan Chalice. Re-cent restoration made necessary by the discovery of dry rot in the pews has given a much more open appearance to this beautiful building. The galleries which surrounded it in Victorian times have long since disappeared and it probably looks much more as it must have looked in earlier centuries, imagining that is, that the comfortable chairs of today are replaced by the simple benches of the time. There is much to see here and a good church guide is on sale. Look for the model of the Tristan da Cunha boat, presented by one of those Islanders who made their home in Fawley for some years after they were evacuated from the Island when the volcano erupted. Look too for the fragment of an Italian bomb which devastated the chancel in 1940, now so beautifully restored.

An organ was presented to the church in 1867 by Mrs Berkeley Drummond. Before that there had been a small band of strings and no doubt wind instruments. "..Henry Wheeler and his son were repaid for buying strings for the bass viol and the violoncello.." The organ was destroyed when the bomb fell and replaced by one in the West, recently rebuilt over the west door with a separate console in

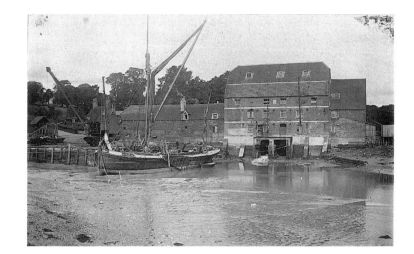

Ashlett Mill with a barge at the quay.

The first passenger train at Fawley station, July 1925.

A victorian watercolour of Fawley Church.

the body of the church. There are interesting memorials inside the church and outside in the churchyard. By the gate is the grave of members of the Cossor family, one a pioneer in radio production.

In 1839 a complete land survey was made of the parish and it tells us that Fawley village and the nearby hamlet of Rhimehall were of about equal size. The Church, the old Rectory, a gateway to the Cadland Estate with its lodge-keepers cottage and the earlier *Falcon Inn* next door marked the southern end of Fawley itself, with Church Farm a little nearer the shore. A deed of 1779 relates to "The Falcon Inn, late the New Inn, heretofore the Ship" It must have had at least one large room since vestry meetings were held there and Justices of the Peace used it occasionally as a court. That earlier Fawley was connected to Rhimehall by the present Church Lane, then a tree-lined way with just three or four thatched cottages along it. Over the years the village centre moved southwards and is now the present Fawley Square. Hardly an imposing open space, but surrounded by interesting buildings, and the heart of village life since then.

Fawley Jubilee Hall was built by public subscription in 1887 to mark Queen Victoria's Golden Jubilee, soon after its completion a clock and bell was installed as a monument to the Reverend Hoare and in 1897 it was extended to mark the Queen's Diamond Jubilee. In the first half of this century it was the centre of village entertainment by local Dramatic Societies and the scene of many political debates at election time. It was extensively renovated in the 1950's and added to in more recent years so that today it houses the Fawley Library, the Parish Council Offices and in a modern annexe has two up-to-date Squash courts and a viewing gallery.

14th Century Silver patten and Elizabethan chalice.

To return to 1887, the Drummond scrapbooks contain a detailed account in a newscutting of the time, of the laying of the foundation stone of the hall by Miss Drummond of Cadland.

..Precisely at 6.30 a procession was formed and left the Rectory ground for the site....(The order of the procession is given in detail)...on arrival the procession was met by Mr E.A.Drummond JP, Miss Drummond and Miss Edith Drummond, and a vast crowd of villagers numbering nearly 400...The band played, and then the Old Hundredth hymn was sung, after which the chairman offered up a short prayer, – Miss Drummond next proceeded to lay the stone, bearing the following inscription: "This foundation stone was laid by Miss Drummond, of Cadland, 17th May, 1887". Having done so, she declared the stone to be well and truly laid, amidst loud cheering. The trowel, a very handsome one, was presented by Mr E.W. Unwin, the triangle (a level) and mallet were made from walnut cut on the Cadland estate, "highly finished and polished".

The foundation stone is still there, on the right as you approach the modern aluminium doors, the "very handsome trowel" is in the Parish Clerk's office inside, the "highly polished walnut triangle and mallet" are perhaps still with the Drummond family.

Next door but one to the Jubilee Hall is a building, now the Sir Galahad restaurant, which has been many things in its time. We uncovered the date stone of 1739 when rebuilding the front in 1971 and also found the reveals of the downstairs windows of the original cottage. From the Bill of Sale (see p.43) one can see that in 1883 it was already a shop with bakehouse, stables, garden and other land, a thriving business no doubt. In about 1900 the photograph shows it as the general village store, still a bakery, but with household wares in the bay windows. In 1953 when we moved our first pharmacy there, the shop sold confectionery and tobacco, was an off-licence, and stocked cycle spares as well. It still has traces of its past in the space where the bread oven was, the hooks for rails on which meat was hung and the stone sets of the stable floor.

Further down the road is a Building Company's offices where Mr Giles's general store at the corner of Ashlett and Calshot roads, supplied bread, cakes, groceries, beer, drapery, ironmongery and even Pratt's Motor Spirit. He owned the first car in the

Church Lane, looking towards Fawley Square.

Fawley about 1900.

area and an elderly resident reminisced of the time when as a girl of twelve or thirteen, her brother George ran into their house shouting for them to come out and see something coming along the road with no horses! It was travelling from the direction of Beaulieu, and we know from a daughter of Mr. Giles that he used to meet Lord Montagu in his Daimler along the road across the heath at Hilltop, when they compared notes on their cars' performances.

The business was later owned by Williamson and Treadgold and was part of the Misselbrook and Weston group until larger stores and supermarkets came to the Waterside. Fawley has always been too small for these larger developments and still has its own local traders for its immediate needs.

Opposite the restaurant on the other corner is another converted house which the Hayward family kept as the butcher's shop for many years, it was a part of the premises mentioned in a lease of 1675 as the Blue Anchor Inn.

Next door, the Florist's shop was originally a cottage where the Caton family were the village saddlers and harness makers for a long period. Peter Caton's will of 1828 is in the Cadland Estate papers and his son, James Caton, is in a Hampshire Directory of 1859. He appears with his family in the 1871 census but died in 1891 and by 1911, the business had passed to the William Simmonds seen in the photograph. In 1927 the Carnival photograph shows that the front shop has been divided into two, the first office of the National Provincial and Union Bank and 'The Chocolate Box' The saddler at that time still worked from a small part of the back of the building and his shop window can be seen at the side.

Plaque uncovered at pharmacy, Fawley.

The present *Falcon Hotel* dates from about 1850. Mr Waterman was the first licensee; his son who succeeded him, is on the left of the front cover photograph of about 1900. The grandson, speaking of his father, remembered that

> ..A bottle of whisky cost sixteen shillings then and he charged three to deliver it to Cadland... Opening hours in those days were from 6 am to 10 pm and men would call in for a breakfast pint on their way to work

At this time the *Falcon* was also a farm and his father

> ..used to buy a thousand sheep at Wilton Fair and arrange for a drover to walk with them to the Bold Forester at Marchwood. A postcard from Totton on the previous day would enable him to be there to drive them home...Bullocks were driven to Brockenhurst Market via Beaulieu, leaving Fawley on Wednesday and arriving for the Thursday market, together with the lambs and pigs which had left Fawley at four o'clock that morning

Mr Fred Cole moved from Hythe to Fawley in 1897 with his family and established a builder's business at Laurel Cottage. There was a large yard and outbuildings adjacent and he built many of the pre-war houses in the village, including those in Coleville Avenue nearby.

In 1910 he and his wife opened a new Post Office in an extension to Laurel Cottage. The earliest reference to a Post Office in Fawley that we have is dated 1859. This is in the Gazetteer and Directory of Hampshire and Isle of Wight which notes that it ".... is at Mr. John Johnston's in Fawley where money orders are granted and paid. Letters received and dispatched by mail cart via Southampton". By 1881 George Giles had become postmaster. William Major followed him with the post office in his own home at Malthouse Farm which was on the corner of Copthorne Lane and next to the Jubilee Hall where the Squash courts are now. Kelly's Directory of 1911 lists "Post mail office and telegraph office in Fawley. Frederick Cole postmaster. Letters received through the Southampton office at 6am. and 3.55pm".

Mr. Coles' second daughter Doris returned to live in Fawley and was able to remember that her parents opened the new post office, the very day that Doris' elder sister Ruby left school at fourteen years af age

PARTICULARS.

THE EXCELLENT AND COMPACT

BUSINESS PREMISES,

PLEASANTLY SITUATE

AT FAWLEY, IN THE COUNTY OF HANTS,

Now sold for the last twenty-five years in the occupation of Mr. Edmund Blunden, Baker and Grocer, a Yearly Tenant, at £30 per annum.

The Property comprises a BRICK-AND-TILED

DWELLING HOUSE WITH DOUBLE-FRONTED SHOP

Sitting-Room behind, 3 Bedrooms, a small Bedroom, Lumber Room, &c., also a Store (adjoining the Shop),

A CAPITAL BAKEHOUSE

With Baker's Oven, Kitchen, Pantry, Yard, with Pump of good Water, &c.

There is a good side entrance, which leads to a STORE (timber-built with tiled roof), and an excellent brick-and-slated

TWO-STALL STABLE WITH LOFT OVER,

Also a

Timber-and-Tiled CART SHED,

Piggery, and other Buildings; adjoining is

A PRODUCTIVE GARDEN

and at the rear is a

GOOD PIECE OF ARABLE LAND

The whole lying well together, and containing, by estimation, about 1½ Acres.

The Property is Copyhold of the Manor of Bitterne; a Tenure nearly (if not quite) equal to Freehold.

See page 40.

Mr Giles's store before 1908.

The butcher's shop about 1900.

The saddler's next door.

Mr. Wheeler and Jesse South as a child in 1909.

Fawley Carnival 1927.

Laurel Cottage, now the Post Office.

Fawley School class, 1908.

and went straight into the business. A Miss Raisy who had worked for William Major across the square came to the new premises and her experience was very useful in teaching Ruby (and later Doris), the telegraphy side of the post office work.

Doris remembered Marconi when he lived at Eaglehurst, at that time he was conducting radio experiments from his laboratory in the tower. She was working on the switchboard and would take messages for the Royal Naval Air station (later the R.A.F.) at Calshot delivering them, often at night, on her bicycle. It was Sherbine Moody who then took the mail to Totton travelling in all weathers in an open mailcart drawn by one horse. He stayed overnight at *The Elephant and Castle* returning with mail for Fawley each morning by 5 am. He had a little home in the apple orchard by their yard.

The house called *Meadow View* has an interesting history and former residents have been able to help us to record some of it. Hampshire Constabulary were the first people known to have rented the cottage belonging at that time to the Cadland Estate. It might have been the police house as early as 1890 when Joseph Isaacson was police constable for Fawley. In 1906 P.C. Barratt and his wife came to the cottage. A year later their first daughter was born there. This daughter recalled her life in the cottage throughout the first World War

> ...I remember when the *Hampshire* went down. The telephones were all morse code in those days and we could hear messages coming in because it was only next door in the Post Office. Mrs Cole came running to tell us the news because Willie Waterman of the Falcon was on board with Lord Kitchener's troops....The first telephone from here went to Beaulieu and when anyone asked Father the way to Beaulieu he used to say 'Follow the wires!'...

P.C. Alexander and his wife came to Meadow View, the Fawley police house in about 1923 and Mrs Alexander recalled

> ...Honestly, there was no candle, no lamp, no range. There was a well in the kitchen and a bread oven. To cook in it you had to put faggots (bundles of sticks) in and light them. Then when it was hot enough, you raked out the faggots, wiped the floor of the oven and put in the bread. Cadland Estate used to provide us with wood for it but we never used it. Dad

wasn't satisfied so Fred Cole said that he'd buy it (the house) from the Estate and do it up for Dad. He bought it from Mr. Drummond in 1925 and built on a new office out at the back with a bedroom over the top. That was a lovely dry room. He built us our first toilet, before, we'd only had a bucket toilet in the garden. Of course when they built on the new rooms it covered over the window on the landing. I used to like to stand and look out of that window over the garden and the fields behind. A policeman's life was very different in those days. You were really something. The trades people were very kind and each year we had a brace of pheasants from Cadland Estate and one from Exbury...

Beyond *Meadow View*, the way out of the old village is by a lane which is perhaps the best example left of how these roads looked half a century or more ago, tree-lined and shady. In this case they survived because they are oaks and if you look, show how, when as saplings they were damaged by the village lads as one of them admitted to us regretfully in his old age.

Just beyond the avenue on the right is the building which for many years was Fawley School. It was built by the Drummond family in 1840 for the sum of £700. There had been Dame schools in the past supported by the Church or the Drummond family, while in the 17th century the Parish Clerk was required to keep a school for poor children. This newer building provided separate rooms for Boys, Girls and Infants. The school logs which date from 1867 tell us a lot about country children's lives in that latter part of the 19th century. They walked to school from as far as Lepe and Calshot, suffering badly from chilblains and other ailments in Winter and bad weather. From quite an early age they often had to help the family purse out by cow minding, manure carting and at harvest time. These as well as "No boots" are frequent excuses for absence. The most important function of the year was the standard examination in the "Three R's" Only children who had made 200 attendances could sit and the amount of money granted to the school depended on the results as well as the Inspector's report.

Children did however enjoy Sunday School Outings and Chapel Teas, there were also rare visits to the Forest or the seaside, families and groups using horse drawn wagons. The Fawley Band was usually present at special occasions, Harvest Home, or at Christmas entertainment and marching at the head of Carnival processions.

Fawley had one of the oldest Cricket Clubs in the New Forest, and there was a regular fixture with Beaulieu until well after the Second World War. The local newspaper of the time gives an account of the 1867 visit of the Southampton Clarence Club to a match at the Cadland estate against the Fawley team. On a fine day they found the grounds

> ...gaily decorated with flags, and refreshments were served in the conservatory on arrival. Wickets were pitched in a most delightful spot, the game was most pleasant, agreeable and well contested. Those of the visitors not engaged in cricket strolled around the beautiful grounds and enjoyed the magnificent scenery. At the conclusion of the game the cricketers adjourned to a suitable spot where a successful photograph was taken. After this all sat down to a first rate tea presided over by Mrs. Drummond......The day finished with a concert of music and songs followed by the dancing of quadrilles, polkas, schottisches and country dances until the National Anthem was played at eleven o'clock...

Fawley Cricket Club, 1920.

Chapter Four

The Big House at Cadland

In 1772 the Hon. Robert Drummond bought the Manor of Cadland in Fawley from Lady Mary Talbot and her sister, later acquiring some adjoining land at Stone and Stanswood. Robert was the third son of William, 4th Viscount Strathallan of the Drummond family of Scotland. When he was young his father had sent him south, away from the disturbances of the time, to Strathallan's brother Andrew who had a banking business in London. In 1746 the Viscount was killed fighting for the Jacobite cause in that desperate battle fought on the boggy plain of Culloden.

Robert prospered in the Drummond's Bank at Charing Cross and became a Governor in 1769. He enjoyed staying in a small house on his new estate, relaxing from London business life by shooting and fishing in a countryside which reminded him of his native Scotland. The architect Henry Holland and Lancelot 'Capability' Brown the creator of landscapes, were both customers of the bank and in 1775 Robert engaged them to produce plans for, "Building the carcase of his new house at Fawley."

The site chosen for the house was on the crest of a hill with a panoramic view of Southampton Water. It was a modest but dignified marine villa built of local bricks and at the same time the little fishing cottage mentioned earlier was built at Bournehill on the Solent shore.

Robert and his family enjoyed their country residence and lived there in style until his death in 1804. Later that same year his son, Andrew Berkeley Drummond, entertained George III at Cadland when the King was visiting the New Forest. To mark the occasion the King presented a small portrait of himself to Andrew. The story is that the royal visitor was being shown the collection of family pictures when they came to a portrait of Andrew's grandfather, Lord Strathallan who had been killed at Culloden. To spare the King embarrassment, the name plate had been removed, but this made him even more curious and on being told who the subject was and that he had died fighting against the King's grandfather, he remarked generously "They were fine men, would that I had been one of them."

Andrew Berkeley Drummond married Lady Mary Percival, daughter of the 2nd Earl of Egmont. Her brother Spencer Percival was Prime Minister during the time of Wellington's victories in the Peninsular War. The only British Prime Minister to be assassinated, he was shot in the breast on May 11th, 1814, as he entered the House of Commons.

Andrew Robert Drummond succeeded to the estate on the death of his father in 1833. His wife was Lady Elizabeth Manners, daughter of the 5th Duke of Rutland. Needing more room for their growing family they decided to enlarge the house and engaged Sir Jeffrey Wyatville, the architect who had guided alterations at Windsor Castle. However, Wyatville's elaborate plans were rejected by Andrew Robert who made himself responsible for the main design of the interior, his object being "To have as plain and simple, but as substantial a house as was possible."

Through his agent and the Clerk of the Works he kept a close watch on the building for which Wyatville only provided the drawings. Dry rot found in the earlier house caused him to build-in metal braces, use iron rather than timber over the windows, to include as little wood as possible generally and omit all lath and plaster-work in the house. Although the interior was quite plain, great attention was paid to the convenience of the layout to provide a happy atmosphere for both family and visitors.

Horses and the hunt, Andrew Robert's great

Cadland Park, *in Hampshire, the* Seat *of* Rob.t Drummond *Esq.r*

Published as the Act directs, Sep.t 5.th 1780, by W.Watts, Kemp's Row, Chelsea.

Cadland House.

Cadland House, early this century.

THEATRE ROYAL, CADLAND.

Unprecedented Attraction !!!
CROWDED HOUSES !!!
THOUSANDS OF POUNDS TURNED AWAY FROM THE DOOR NIGHTLY.

☞ In consequence of one of the principal Actors being called away, " Cool as a Cucumber " cannot be represented.

On WEDNESDAY, December 23, 1863,

LADY ELIZABETH's Servants will perform the Farce of

B. B.

Squire Greenfield	LORD JOHN HERVEY
Bob Rattles (the Ex-Chicken, a retired Prize Fighter)	CAPTAIN ALFRED DRUMMOND
Joe (Waiter at the Percy Arms	MR. CECIL DRUMMOND (late prima donna assoluta of the T.R. Malta
Mr. Benjamin Bobbin (an Agent)	COLONEL H. P. STUART WORTLEY
Mrs. Puncheon (Landlady of the Percy Arms)	LADY JOHN MANNERS
Dorothy (Housemaid at the Percy Arms	HON. MRS. EDGAR DRUMMOND

No Babies or Bonnets allowed in the Stalls, owing to the crowded state of the house; only the Patent Compressible Crinolines can be admitted.

Performance to commence at Nine o'clock precisely.   No money returned.

Stage Manager   —   —   Mr. CECIL DRUMMOND. | Machinist   —   —   Mr. CORBYN.
Costumieres   —   —   Mesdames STROUD and JENNINGS.

VIVAT ELIZABETHA !!

HAMPSHIRE STEAM PRINTING WORKS: R. B. KING, SOUTHAMPTON.

passions, were shared with his father-in-law the Duke of Rutland. Their horse 'Cadland' won the Derby in 1828 after a dead heat was declared between it and 'Colonel'. A re-run took place and 'Cadland' was the victor. Drummond was the Captain Commandant of the New Forest Yeomanry in which he took a very lively interest and he was instrumental in reviving the New Forest Hunt. As a Ranger of the New Forest, Deputy Lieutenant and High Sheriff of Hampshire, he was naturally interested in all local affairs.

He and Lady Elizabeth hosted many splendid occasions at Cadland House. A feature of their Christmas festivities were performances at 'The Theatre Royal – Cadland'. We don't know exactly when these family theatricals began, certainly as early as 1849, for a drawing of the cast that year is in the Drummond scrapbooks, along with printed playbills and programmes of many productions down the years to about 1885.

In Victorian times entertainment for everyone in all walks of life was very much home-made, and at Christmas or party times charades were a very popular way of bringing everyone into the fun of the evening. In the larger estates like Cadland where Christmas was often a large gathering of near and distant relations, distinguished guests, and even royalty, these productions were on a more elaborate scale to involve many of the family and to entertain the company as well as the staff and estate workers.

The Theatre Royal, Cadland was famed for its presentations, which seem to have been predominantly comedies or farces, hardly what we would think of as traditional Christmas plays. These festivities were reported in the press in great detail, and the account of one such Christmas in 1859, gives us a flavour of an early Victorian evening at The Theatre Royal. The account first lists some thirty distinguished guests entertained at Cadland including His Excellency the Prussian Ambassador Count Bernstorff, the Countess Bernstorff and other people of note; it then goes on to mention that on the Monday evening a grand ball was given, many of the leading gentry of the county being present.

> On Wednesday the usual theatrical representation took place, the spacious entrance hall being tastefully fitted up as a theatre, having choice exotics and other decorations of a floral character. The performance in the comic drama *Our Wife* was most spirited, and sustained by the entire corps with unflagging energy to the end; that of Miss Wortley, as

Rosine, Earl Jermyn, as Marquis de Ligny, and Mr. Aidé as the Count de Brissac, equal to any of the metropolitan dramatic professionals. In the farce, *Betsy Baker*, Captain Drummond, in his two characters, and Miss Ricardo, as the intriguing washerwoman, were irresistible. Mr. Baillie Cochrane, as Mr. Grumley, and Mr. Ricardo as Joey in the concluding farce, *Domestic Economy* elicited roars of laughter. The epilogue (as a tête-à-tête between Earl Jermyn and Mr. Aidé) being personally although somewhat indirectly addressed to the Lady Elizabeth and the principal personages of the brilliant assembly, has of course no public interest; suffice it to say that it was one of Mr. Baillie Cochrane's happiest efforts. Refreshments were laid out in the dining-room and library, and the numerous guests and the audience generally must have been highly gratified at the kind and polite attention paid to them by Mr. and the Lady E. Drummond. The dresses and equipments were supplied by Nathan, of Tichbourne-street, London; and we need scarcely add were splendid.

There were other, perhaps less splendid times, when Cadland was host to parochial occasions and country festivals, when the family came together with the staff and workers on the estate farms. In 1863 a newspaper account of thanksgiving for the harvest sets the scene.

> ...All assembled at 10 o'clock, the appointed hour, at the National School and the call was responded to by a large number of persons bearing bouquets of wheat and flowers. A procession was formed, preceded by a corn trophy with the inscription "God giveth the increase" and the Fawley Brass Band, marched to Fawley Church which was profusely and tastefully decorated for the occasion by the Rectors' family....

Harvest Home at Cadland the previous year was a more elaborate celebration and there is a long press account of speeches followed by,

> ...the dining room was decorated with wheat sheaves; in the dairy sheaves were also placed adorned with forty varieties of roses. Tea was provided for a large number of females in a marquee erected in the park. Near this place provision was made for archery, football – a

prolific source of fun and enjoyment, cricket (The Cadland cricketers being in their picturesque dress), throwing for snuff-boxes, 'Aunt Sally', running for dresses, ribands etc., jumping in sacks, and two pigs with greasy tails being let loose became the property of their active captors. Mr Corbin, foreman of the carpenters, had the management of this portion of the proceedings. Dancing commenced about 6 o'clock and was carried on with great spirit until nine. There was a remarked absence of anything like intemperance throughout the day.

The Drummonds had responsibilities in the community at large, as well as to those in their own service. A teacher at Fawley school noted in the log books that the children, particularly those from large families, looked undernourished. For several years it is recorded that in the winter months, school was closed on one afternoon a week to allow a number of children to fetch soup from Cadland. At Christmas, members of the Cadland Penny Clothing Club attended, "...at Cadland for the purpose of receiving from the hands of Mr and Lady Elizabeth Drummond the various articles selected for their use. They afterwards partook of dinner". Clothes were also distributed at the school by Lady Elizabeth as prizes for good work.

On the death of her husband in 1865 she moved to the cottage at Bournehill but maintained her caring interest in the people of the parish. Edgar Atheling Drummond, her second son, succeeded to the Cadland Estate and his father's interest in Drummond's Bank. He had until then made a career at sea and whilst serving as officer of the watch on *H.M.S. Daedalus* during her voyage from the Cape of Good Hope to St Helena in August 1848, recorded the sighting of a 'sea serpent'. When subsequently reported it was said to be, '...the best recorded sighting of such a monster to this day'. His journal describes it thus

> In the 4 to 6 watch at about 5 o'clock, we observed a most remarkable fish on our lee quarter, moving now and then, in a S.W.

Edgar Atheling Drummond's drawing of H.M.S. Daedelus and the 'sea serpent' reported in 1848.

In Cadland grounds.

Jonathan Down, the Cadland shepherd and his family in front of their estate house.

Mr Pike, an estate worker with his ploughing team.

direction. The appearance of its head which, with the back fin, was the only portion of the animal visible, was, long, pointed, and flattened at the top, perhaps about ten feet in length, the upper jaw projecting considerably like a shark's. The fin was perhaps 20 feet in the rear of the head and visible occasionally. The Captain also asserted that he saw the tail, or a second fin, about the same distance behind it. The upper part of the head and shoulders appeared of a dark brown colour and beneath the under jaw a brownish white. It pursued a steady course, keeping the head horizontal in the surface of the water, and in a rather raised position, disappearing occasionally beneath a wave for a very brief interval. It was going at the rate of perhaps 15 miles per hour, and when nearest was perhaps 100 yards distant. In fact it gave one quite the appearance of a large snake or eel, and is probably the same animal which has long been regarded as fabulous, but whose existence has been certified by many respectable eye-witnesses. No one in the ship had ever seen anything similar before, so it is at least

The 1897 Cadland presentation mug and medallion.

extraordinary. In the Captain's opinion it was not less than 120 feet long; I should not have thought above 60 feet, but his eye is quicker and better to judge of distances, which will account for the disparity of estimation.

Fawley Band at Cadland House – before 1914.

Cadland Hospital, September 1914.

Cadland Hospital, Kitchener's ward in the Library.

For nearly thirty years during Edgar's ownership Cadland was perhaps at its best. An estate notebook describes it at this time,

> The farm and farmyard were a perfect model, the rows of cow-sheds with Alderney cows being spotless. The dairy with its wedgewood pans full of cream was quite a picture. On a working day the farmyard was a busy hive with the humming of the steam engine engaged in threshing or driving the sawmill. The musical sound of the blacksmith's hammer, the carpenter and his mate busy upon some piece of furniture, usually a new bookcase and the plumber in his paint shop. There was the bricklayer and the drainer who I never saw without earthenware pipes under his arm, like some badge of office. The dairyman with his old-fashioned pail carriers on his shoulders and his wife in a sun-bonnet, and print dress, busy with her butter making. The wagons with their loads would be coming in at the end of the day to add to the rickyard, already nearly full with its great stacks. The granaries would be replete with their store of threshed corn and oats.... Those were the days when a country gentleman lived entirely on his own produce and such produce too; when everyone seemed cheerful and contented under a benevolent master.... children curtsied on their way to school, the men and boys touched their hats respectfully and in short, it seemed that whatever happened in the world, Cadland was founded upon a rock of well-being and happiness.

This was in the time of England's agricultural heyday; the poor Forest soil of Robert's day had reaped the reward of years of good husbandry and would continue to do so. Edgar had married Louisa Pennington, daughter of the 3rd Lord Muncaster in 1858 and together they added many elegant possessions to the house. He always retained his love of the sea and was a member of the Royal Yacht Squadron. He enjoyed cruising in his yawl *Brunette* and Cadland House was again the venue for special occasions. A

Fourshells, near Blackfield.

Langley, the Post Office about 1925.

newspaper account in August 1881 (probably during Cowes Week) reports a garden party given in the grounds,

> Two large tents were erected in the garden and the band of the 10th Regiment performed a selection of music during the afternoon for a splendid number of distinguished guests. The Cadland Band was stationed at the quay where they played during the afternoon for those of the company who came by water. On the landing of the Prince and Princess of Wales and their suite, the band played 'God Bless the Prince of Wales' Their highnesses were met at the quay by Mr Drummond and his son, Mr Andrew Cecil Drummond and received by Mrs Drummond and her daughters. The National Anthem was played when they left. It was a fine sight to see the yachts in the river, there being some 50 or 60 at one time. A match for a prize off Calshot Castle was being contested for.

The times themselves were changing, Edgar's wife died in 1886 and he in 1893 while on holiday in Venice. Their son Andrew was in poor health and

needed to spend winters abroad. Nevertheless he was devoted to Cadland and in 1897 he provided a happy day for the children of the estate workers to celebrate Queen Victoria's Diamond Jubilee.

> The whole of the children of school age whose parents worked on the Cadland Estate were, through the kindness of Mr A.C. Drummond, given quite a holiday at Bournehill Cottage, situate on the borders of the Solent, which possesses beautiful grounds, and a more suitable spot could not be found. The children, to the number of 108, met at the Public Hall, Fawley, those from Langley and Hardley arriving in waggons. The juveniles having been got in order by Mr Davy, and placed in four waggons, they, headed by the Fawley Brass Band, wended their way to the Cottage, where they arrived about three o'clock, and were received on the lawn by Mr and the Misses Drummond. Mr Drummond addressed the children, and told them that he had invited them there that day, so that they should remember the Queen's Diamond Jubilee, and after a few kind words of welcome, dismissed them to amuse themselves. The Band was stationed on the lawn, and

Mr Nicholas, a worker at Stanswood Farm.

Mr Musselwhite, a carter and thatcher.

Carting furze faggots for Langley brickworks.

played several selections during the afternoon and evening. A large marquee was erected on the lawn, and tastefully decorated with evergreens and flowers by Mr Garner of Cadland gardens. At the back of the marquee was a large Union Jack, and in front of the same, hung an engraving of Her Majesty in her young days. It certainly was high holiday for the children. Some played cricket, but the beach and water were the greatest attraction and treat. It was soon seen that it would be hard not to please them, for they thoroughly enjoyed the balmy sea breezes and the glorious view which extends from Portsdown Hill to the Needles, and the animated scene on the lawn, with its lines of gay bunting and the happy smiling faces of the children, was one not to be easily forgotten. Just before five the whole of the children were mustered and marched into the marquee, the band playing a lively march as the children took their places. A surprise awaited them, as opposite each child's plate was placed a splendid button-hole of flowers, made up in three colours, viz., red, white, and blue. After these had been fastened on and grace sung, the main work was commenced, and thoroughly carried out, till all seemed satisfied. Several photographs of the children were taken during the afternoon by Miss J. Drummond. A large number of the mothers had reached the beach, near the cottage, and these were invited to see the children have tea, and after all were satisfied they also partook of tea which was supplied by Mr A. Major of Fawley, and gave entire satisfaction. Just before seven o'clock the children were mustered on the lawn, and formed two lines. Mr Drummond again spoke a few kind words to them, stating how pleased he was to have them there, and he hoped that they had all enjoyed their day. He asked them to sing "God Save The Queen", which was done heartily, the band accompanying. After this, each child was presented with a mug and a medallion of the Queen. The mug had on one side two profiles representing the Queen in 1837 and 1897, and on the other side a view of Cadland House. Mr Davy requested the children to give three cheers to Mr Drummond for his kindness in inviting them there and giving them such a treat. The youngsters at once broke out into loud applause, which was repeated again and again. Mr Drummond accompanied the children to the waggons, and,

amidst the renewed cheers, as one waggon after the other left, he wished them a safe journey home. Fawley Hall was reached soon after eight o'clock, when the children with cheers dispersed for their homes, those for Hardley and Langley going on in the wagons allotted for that purpose. The band played 'God Save The Queen' and this brought to a close a Jubilee treat which will ever be remembered by the children.

Andrew Cecil retired to the cottage and in 1911 leased Cadland to his brother Maldwin, who three years before, had married an American heiress, Albertine, widow of Marshall Field Jnr. of Chicago and she was able to support the increasingly heavy expenses of the estate. When War broke out in 1914 Maldwin joined his old regiment, a battalion of the 60th Rifles; while his wife made Cadland House a military hospital for the wounded. She herself was the Commandant and men in 'hospital blues' became a familiar sight in Fawley. She became ill and died at her task in 1916.

Mr Lowe, the estate farrier.

After the war, in the face of a changed economy, death duties and the great financial depression, Maldwin sold land to the east of the house down to the salt marshes at the water's edge for the building of the original A.G.W.I. (Anglo, Gulf, West Indies Petroleum Corporation) oil refinery in 1920. He had no direct heir and was succeeded by his surviving brother Cyril Augustus in 1929. Other land had to be sold to the Crown for barrack buildings at Eaglehurst near Calshot. Meanwhile, Bournehill Cottage had suffered another disastrous fire and lay neglected until rebuilding began in 1934 when Cyril Drummond decided to leave the big house at Cadland and move to this much more convenient home on the Solent shore.

The old house was let as a country club and in the Second World War it became a corps headquarters. Afterwards, it and the land around was sold to become the site of the present Esso oil refinery and soon the 'Big House' was no more.

Today, as we drive down the road to Fawley and Calshot we can still see the twin Lodges at the north-west entrance which led to the house, now framing a view of the refinery, but passing it on our left, are spared much of its impact by the tree screen which was planted in 1950, incorporating some remnants of the old estate woodlands. In spring it re-creates a memory of an earlier time when bluebells still carpet the ground under the trees and create a brilliant river of blue. At the turn of the century, little Ivy Maton after an illness, was sent by her father and mother to live with her grandparents at the Cadland Home Farm, where her grandmother was in charge of the dairy and responsible for regular supplies to the family, whether at home or at their London residence. Ivy attended Fawley village school, recovered in the clean country air, and in her eighties, still remembered how she enjoyed the primroses and bluebells on her walk home to the farm through the woods of the house.

Around the Cadland Estate were small groups of cottages such as those at Langley and Blackfield on the edges of Blackwell and Hughes Commons. These were virtually unchanged until early this century when it was still a predominantly rural community. The advent of industry from the first refinery on the shore to the petro-chemical complex of today with its ancillaries and small industrial estates, has changed these places radically. In 1928, the sale of land in Langley, Rollestone and Holbury belonging to the Sloane-Stanley Estate, which had been part of the Manor of Cadland until 1657, released large areas for homes to be built. Since then both private and local authority housing estates with shops, community buildings and churches have transformed these original hamlets into thriving residential areas.

Shelley's Off-Licence at Blackfield Crossroads, 1934.

Chapter Five

Holbury, Hardley and Butts Ash

Holbury was a manor in the 14th Century, licenced by the King to the Abbey of Beaulieu until the monasteries were finally dissolved. After this the earliest surviving rating lists show in the 1600s a number of farms, including Hardley, Little Holbury and Great Holbury, each with a few cottages near the farmhouse.

Henry Audley, the Receiver General, died at one of these farms in 1606 and left to his wife Cicely the remainder of certain leases on trust, for her to pay the rents to the parishes of Eling, Fawley and Whitchurch, where lands formed part of his estate. Although sole heiress to the rest of his fortune, his wife objected to parting with this money so she

Long Lane Holbury – Beaulieu Lodge at Kennels corner.

married the executor of his will and together they defrauded the beneficiaries for seven years. The churchwardens and overseers of the three parishes however won their case and the money was eventually paid to them until the leases expired.

The records of the law suit and the charity accounts in the Fawley parish papers, show that the 'Colhendy Money', which was used to provide schooling for poor children, was often in dispute.

Holbury Manor itself is a site of very early occupation. Earlier excavation nearby revealed stone foundations of medieval buildings with floor-tile fragments similar to those at Beaulieu and there was some evidence that it may have been a moated site. Thomas Pace, who gained lands at the time of the dissolution of the Abbey refers in his will of 1559 to, "...my new house at Holbury..."

The Holbury Manor Farmhouse, much altered and added to, may have been that house. A recent owner, Mr Wiltshire, had a large collection of artefacts found on the farm over many years, of Romano-British or earlier date, which are now with the Hampshire County Museum Service. In 1971 the farmhouse and 12 acres of land were sold to a property developer and the building was made the subject of a preservation order. When new houses were being built more evidence of early occupation came to light including a hearth site, with charcoal and metal waste, which we were able to photograph, but unfortunately there was no time for further excavation.

Fire badly damaged the house in 1972, but the remains are to be incorporated in new dwellings, and surrounded by other new homes. Part of the former farmland is also a recreation area created by the developers for the Fawley parish as an open space and play area for children.

Reputedly haunted, Old Holbury Mill, off Lime Kiln Lane has an uncertain history and is probably not the original mill building. The parish archives mention it as having been built in 1651 and, "...rented to Lambert for three lives at 1..2s..0d". (Three lives were those of the tenant and the next two members of the family to hold the property. After the third death a new lease was made.)

Long Lane, Holbury is on the line of the lane

The Agwipets concert party.

which joined Fawley with Hythe before today's road. There were only a few houses along it opposite the tree-lined boundary of the Cadland Estate.

Now this busy stretch of the A326 is lined with shops and behind these are streets and houses. At about the centre of Long Lane is the Esso Recreation Club and playing fields, built originally for the workers of the old (AGWI) refinery and enlarged greatly in 1951 when the new refinery came. Next to it is the Waterside Cinema, actually part of the recreation club with a large well-equipped stage which has ensured the continuation of the theatrical tradition of shows, plays and musicals in this part of the Waterside.

When Doctor Eric Jones Evans started a quiet country practice just outside Fawley in 1922 it was a, "Sleepy little village".

His rounds were made on horseback and what his patients did not know was that their doctor had been a professional actor, a film 'extra', a student and lover of Dickens' works and a lifelong friend of many prominent stage people. They might never have known he said,

> Had I not rashly consented to recite a dramatic monologue bearing the lurid title, The Pigtail of Li Fang Hoo as an item in the entertainment that followed one of the annual Harvest Suppers. Seduced by the applause, I sang in dialect two yokel numbers – Oi've come oop from Zummerzet and The Village Pump as an encore. I lived to regret it! Or did I? From that evening's lapse I was roped in for every possible charity and fund raising show.

Indeed in one year he appeared on stage in Fawley Hall a dozen times, presenting monologues, characters from Shakespeare and selections from his quick-change Dickensian scenes. This led to the formation of the 'Agwipets', a concert party mainly recruited from the office staff of the AGWI Company plus talented locals. Jones Evans produced the shows, selected the items and wrote any extra material needed. He described the members of his company as,

> A happy, hard-working group with great talent: Cyril Bristow – a born comedian whose timing was perfect; Kenneth David – a fine vocalist and no mean exponent of the terpsichorean art; Harold Newton – a virtuoso who, had he chosen, could have made a small fortune tickling the ivories in West End cabaret.

The three ladies, Nancy Curtis, A. Humphries and Pat Adkins were eye-catching glamour girls who could high-kick, shuffle and tap with professional ease and put over vocal numbers in style.

The company of seven, dressed in their lavender coloured Pierrot costumes with ruffles, pom-poms and black silk head scarves, charmed audiences all over the Waterside, Southampton, Winchester and beyond. They adapted the show to suit any stage or theatre, playing to enthusiastic audiences and raising money for many deserving causes. All this prompted the formation of the AGWI Dramatic Society in 1927 and with Jones Evans' help and advice on stagecraft and acting, Irving's *The Bells* was performed in the following November, the first of many such productions. Jones Evans himself formed another company in 1933 which used as its theatre the Womens' Institute hall at Dibden Purlieu. Again, except for two other professionals, all involved were amateurs, for he always maintained that with patience, strict discipline and hard work, "They are capable of attaining standards comparable to those of a first class provincial repertory company".

He was by then the refinery's doctor but later abandoned his medical career to return to the professional stage, playing opposite Bransby Williams and Phyllis Neilson-Terry and taking his one man Dickens show on tour in this country, then in Holland and Germany.

The Esso Music and Drama group followed these successes in the new Cinema/Theatre in 1950 with *The Chiltern Hundreds* and Edward German's opera, *Merrie England* the following year. Each year since then they have produced plays, shows and pantomimes to a very high standard. Near the cinema are the buildings of Hardley School, which has its own stage and a long history of school plays for public audiences. It also became the venue for the Waterside Operatic Society whose first production there was Gilbert and Sullivan's *Iolanthe* in 1968, succeeded by other G & S operettas until 1972 when Franz Lehar's *The Merry Widow* was a sell-out. Two years later came an amateur first, *The Savoyards*, an ambitious staging of the story of the Savoy theatre, its composer and librettist and their turbulent relationship, written by Donald Madgwick and set to the best-loved music of their shows by Stanford Robinson. In 1978, the company were able to use the stage of the Waterside cinema for larger scale musicals such as *Viva Mexico* and *Fiddler On The Roof* to alternate yearly with G & S favourites.

Hardley. Schools.

Hardley School, pre 1900.

To complete the story of Eric Jones Evans, who had to retire from acting because of arthritis in 1963 but continued writing plays for the stage and appeared on television in programmes based on his life. His collection of memorabilia of the Victorian and Edwardian stages was exhibited several times at the Russell-Cotes Art Gallery. He died in 1989 at more than 90 years old, an unforgettable figure as we remember him, stepping with a flourish of his black, wide-brimmed hat and large flowing cape, out of his car – into an imaginary spotlight – for as he said, "I am an actorr!"

Hardley School, now becoming independent and self-governing at the start of 1991 was formerly a comprehensive and at another time a secondary-modern school. It was opened in 1935 and Ted Mudge, son of the Waterside's own photographer and then a new boy, remembers it vividly,

"It seemed very strange to come into a completely new building for the first time, and to see the quadrangle in the centre. I don't think I had even heard the word before, let alone seen one... Exciting, but at the same time rather frightening to meet all at once, and for the first time, so many new fellow pupils, from places which seemed to us far afield, from Marchwood in the north to the country villages of Exbury and Lepe in the south...I remember that it took some time before we were organised into classes, and I think that I joined Form III under the direction of Miss Andrews, a very pleasant teacher. I do remember how cold the classrooms were that morning as the boiler was not yet working properly!

Beyond the 'Quad' was the Boys' wood-work room under the watchful eye of Mr. Newton, and on the other side the girls were taught cookery by Miss Tate. Between these two rooms was the Laboratory where Mrs. Drake tried hard to teach us the rudiments of Science. Our head master was Mr. McKay, a rather dour Scot who kept everyone in order, often forcibly. The Deputy-head Mr. Jimmy Dedman was just the opposite, a kindly soul, who would sometimes shorten lessons by reminiscing of the times he had spent in India. Two other

London Lodge gates, main entrance to Cadland Park.

The Fawley Flyer at Lowe's Bottom and the entrance gates to Forest Lodge.

teachers I remember with affection were Miss Huber and Mr Budge, no doubt there were others, but perhaps affection is not the right word for some of them.

That school was the successor to the old Hardley School set up by the Drummond family in 1869. The building itself was in the style of the estate lodge houses and survives today (alongside the Pinewood Café) with its distinctive, decorative barge-boards to the gables. Kelly's Directory of 1911 describes it as being "...for girls and infants...with 59 children and an average attendance of 42, Mrs Marvin the schoolmistress".

Memories of the war years are still fresh in the minds of the older people of Hardley and Holbury. Behind them in Lime Kiln Lane, where the caravan park now stands was an anti-aircraft battery, the first in the Southampton area to be equipped with radar; the sound of its four 4.5" guns dominated the nights when German raiders attacked Southampton itself and bombs straddled the Waterside. In Frost Lane farm lived the Martin sisters, one of whom kept a diary from 1928 to 1967 and recorded the night of Sunday November 17th, 1940,

> More heavy rain today. Our cellar is flooded and the land around the ricks is covered with water. Raid on Southampton last night. Siren again at 7.00pm. Bombs falling not very far away.

Monday 18th November 1940. Raid continued until 7.00am this morning. Bombs dropped at Hythe, Hardley, Holbury, Beaulieu and Southampton. Damage done to buildings and the roof and 8 ceilings of a house at Hardley by a bomb in the garden and nine in nearby fields. Two bungalows hit in Springfield Grove (Holbury) and some houses in Shore Road. (Hythe) A lot of houses have broken windows. Mr Renyard killed by a bomb that made a crater in the main road near the Pinewood Tea Rooms. About 12 injured in Hythe and Holbury.

What the diary did not record was that a bomb had hit the gun site and killed several soldiers.

The Old School House was at that time divided into three and in one part lived Pamela Lowe, a pupil at Hardley School. Pamela, now Mrs Talbot recalls,

> It was a very bad night when the stick of bombs was dropped on the anti-aircraft site, through the fields and copse between the Methodist Church and our house, the last one landing out on the main road. Mother and I were indoors in our large larder that was in the middle of the house. My father, with a Holbury policeman and Mr Renyard were outside the house as this was their assembly point when the sirens sounded. When the bombs dropped father came in and said that Mr Renyard had been

Forest Lodge, from the lakeside.

killed. We picked up our things, coats and a case of valued possessions and went to the school air raid shelters. After that we went to the school shelters many times. When we got back after that bomb the middle section of the Old School building was in rather a mess as all the windows had been broken. Only the ceiling of our living room was down and a piece of shrapnel had gone through a window and pierced the gas mantle on the other side of the dining room. There was a lot of dust and we had to have our breakfast in the midst of it.

One of Mr Renyard's daughters told us that he was a special constable and also the local blacksmith. They lived at the forge in the cottages by what is now Hardley roundabout. He is remembered on the war memorial plaque in All Saint's Church, Fawley with other civilians and members of the armed forces.

Leaving Hardley by the roundabout, the A326 skirts the boundary of the New Forest and leads directly northwards out of the Waterside, another new road towards the water serves the ancillary industries of the petrochemical complex and between them the way to Hythe follows the line of the old road. On the left of this is Netley View estate, here the road has been straightened and re-graded, hiding a former dip in it, once known as Lowe's Bottom, on the right.

This is the entrance to Forest Lodge and a gazetteer of 1859 records George Robbins living there with his family. When the Hampshire Police force was formed in 1839, Captain George Robbins was appointed the first Chief Constable. The initial recruits were often unsuited for the duties required of them but his military discipline improved the standard and later entrants were required to be smart in appearance and of good behaviour, with a warning not to get drunk, "...especially at gatherings such as fairs where temptation is great"!

Kelly's Directory of 1911 describes Forest Lodge,

The house, originally built in 1730 and recently enlarged has attached grounds and lands of about 100 acres containing a small lake; the land is undulating, heavily timbered and affords fine views; the grounds have a chinese pagoda used as a dining room, a chinese bridge and boathouse: The observatory which stands 200 feet above sea level commands an extensive view, including the town of Southampton, the River Itchen, The New Forest, Hythe and Calshot Castle.

Forest Lodge was also home to the Waterside's only holder of the Victoria Cross, Commander Edward Unwin V.C. It was awarded for his heroism at the landing on 25th April 1915 on 'V' beach at Gallipoli in the Dardenelles campaign.

He proposed a way of landing a large number of men from a specially prepared ship which was to be run up onto the heavily defended beach. The *River Clyde* was chartered, Unwin was put in command and modified her in ways startlingly like those used in 1944 in the D-day landings. Machine guns on her foc'sle behind steel plates gave covering fire. Ports, covered by flaps were cut in her sides, from these troops could pour out onto platforms leading forward and down gangways to a series of lighters alongside which as soon as the *River Clyde* grounded would be a pontoon bridge to the beach. In this way it was hoped to land 2,500 troops quickly to support others going ahead in small boats, to overpower the defences and link up with other forces landing on adjacent beaches.

The action was timed for 6.00am but as Unwin had foreseen, defences held their fire until the boats were close in. It was murderously intense and in minutes virtually everyone in the boats was killed or wounded. All now depended on the *River Clyde*. Unwin ran her ashore exactly where intended, but the beach shelved less steeply than expected, the bridge of boats was too short by a few feet and men had to wade ashore into barbed wire and heavy machine-gun cross-fire. One of the lighters swung away leaving a gap and as most of those on her were killed or seriously wounded, Unwin went down himself, stood in water to his waist and with a handful of men, worked to re-position her. For an hour they battled before it was done, whilst hundreds died around them in the attempt to get ashore. Unwin and five others were awarded Victoria Crosses for their heroism that morning.

At the top of the hill we have left Hardley and are in Butts Ash. An ancient name, but the farms, fields and estates of a century ago are now, almost all, covered with houses. Frost Lane leads off to our right and winds down to Shore Road alongside Southampton Water. At Frost Lane Farm in 1851 lived William Bound with his wife, three sons and two daughters, tilling 150 acres with the help of two farm labourers. His neighbours in the lane were the Hawkesworth, Rann, Dumper, Osman, Wain, Orris and Hosey families, names still found in the Waterside today.

At Butts Ash House, Frederick Fry, the Relieving Officer and Registrar for Hythe lived with his mother and two sisters.

Chapter Six

Hythe and Dibden Purlieu

The word Hythe is derived from the Anglo-Saxon, meaning a landing place and the village grew at a point where it was possible to land dry-shod from Southampton Water. Like others on the Waterside shoreline it was also situated near a stream of fresh water, referred to in the Cadland papers as the 'Hythe Bunny'.

For centuries, boatmen from this small fishing hamlet have ferried cargo and passengers to and from the busy port of Southampton. The earliest reference to 'Hitheferye' is on Saxton's map of 1575 and records show that an ancient custom required these ferrymen to deposit one boat load of stones against Southampton town walls within the piles every six months, to reinforce the banks against the action of the tides. Dr Speed, the Southampton historian explains that in 1683, by complying with this order the boatmen were exempted from paying a toll of 4d each time they landed passengers or goods at the port. Although there is a long history of disputes with the town over the dues charged, the first real threat to the ferrymen's trade came in 1830 with the *Emerald*, this, the first steam ferry boat was introduced by W.C. Westlake, and made regular passages

South Street Hythe, on a sunny day late in Victoria's reign.

The Buildings, Hythe, at the bottom of South Street.

between Hythe and Southampton as well as a daily run to and from Cowes on the Isle of Wight.

A wooden hulled paddle steamer of 22 tons, she astonished Hythe people by making the crossing in 11 minutes, or 14 against the tide! The passage to Cowes was the more successful part of the operation and this, coupled with increasing towage duties in the port as well as excursion trips in Southampton Water, put an end to the ferry service which was once again left to the boatmen in their wherries.

There was competition again in 1836 from a purpose-built iron steamboat, *Forester*, owned by Capt. J.H. Knight (Snr.) and Messrs Smith and Company, under the command of Capt. George R. Mason who was the landlord of *The Wheatsheaf* public house, which was also the Packet and ferry office. Again, a regular service started with occasional trips to Beaulieu and Lymington, but by 1840 the ferry traffic had slumped and the service ended by the August of that year.

Up to this time each boat used as a ferry had to be licenced and regulations laid down as to how many people could be carried, but this was done away with by Southampton Harbour Board in 1842. Two years later an Act of Parliament was passed, "...for making a Landing Place at or near Hythe in the Parish of Fawley and extra parochial places adjoining thereto..."

Andrew Robert Drummond had sponsored the Bill and was the leading shareholder in the Hythe Hard Company which was then set up. In the 1600s Hythe had been in two parts and the stream flowed between them through a tidal lagoon to Southampton Water. This gradually filled becoming 'The Marsh' but it still separated the spit of land on which the High Street was built, from the buildings on the shore proper. The stream turned toward the east and ran out through a deep channel at a point to the north of Berry's shop, opposite where the old *Anchor and Hope* public house stood, for in the deeds of the shop site it was declared to be, "...next to the bridge..."

Obviously the stream was forded or bridged and this area has always been referred to as 'The Bridge' although no trace of any structure remains.

However, the new hard was completed within a year of the act being passed. The Company, using half of the land belonging to the former *Wheatsheaf*, channelled the stream through a culvert, re-aligned the first part of the hard and constructed a new L-shaped stone quay. The stream bed alongside was dredged thus allowing larger vessels to berth at from high to medium states of the tide.

Another steam ferry boat, the *Gipsy* used the new quay but again found the long term trade no better than her predecessors. An attempt to persuade users

The Quay and Pier, postmarked 1908.

Mr Wheeler's cab and two others, waiting for customers from the ferry, pre 1900.

The Bridge. The postage stamp on the card is from Edward VII's reign (1901-1910).

and residents to take up shares in an operating Company failed and the service lapsed once more, but in 1855 the Hythe and Southampton Steam Ferry Company with Mr A.R. Drummond and the Duke of Buccleuch as the principal shareholders, was incorporated and bought the *Prince Alfred* paddle steamer to initiate the service until their new ship was built. In 1856 Andrew Drummond's wife duly named her at Hythe, *Lady Elizabeth*, after herself, and with this additional steamer the ferry operated very successfully, but as the years passed complaints about the condition of the hard were made by passengers, "It was a common experience, to have to wait for the tide to go down, or else wade through the water to get to the steamer"

The building of a pier became a priority and plans were drawn up in 1870 for one 2000 feet in length, a tollhouse on the shore and a floating pontoon at the seaward end. There were many difficulties, but for these and a detailed history of the ferry service, you must read Alan Titheridge's book, *Hythe Pier and Ferry*. Suffice it for us to know that the pier was built in 1880, so that Hythe at last had a means of providing a dry landing for passengers and goods at all states of the tide, something that we can still appreciate today, more than a hundred years later. The opening itself on New Year's day 1881 was something of an occasion, for the Mayor of Southampton (Alderman J.H. Cooksey) left Southampton Pier at 2.00 pm in one of the Union Company's Steam Launches, in his capacity as Admiral of the Port, with the Admiralty flag flying and with the insignia of his office, the Mace and the Silver Oar. He was accompanied by

the Sheriff, the Town Clerk, the Borough Surveyor and other members of the Corporation. They were met at the pierhead by Mr Drummond, Lord Henry Scott and other Hythe people. The ceremony was simple, the speeches short, and all adjourned to lunch at *The Drummond Arms*.

In 1887, Mr Fry, lessee of the pier tolls was succeeded by Mr James Percy; so beginning the long and happy association of the Percy family with the pier and ferry which has continued for more than a century since. Their family firm, the General Estates Company, bought the steamers and continued to operate the ferry service from 1915, just before the death of James Percy. He was a direct descendant of Sir Henry Percy, first Earl of Northumberland and father of Harry, called Hotspur, known as 'the small warrior with the great heart' from his valorous deeds in the 14th century. *Hotspur* became the name of the family's ferry boat and four others have followed the first one, a paddle steamer. Today *Hotspur IV, Hythe Hotspur* and *New Forester* are the boats that ply between Hythe and Southampton daily, besides taking many visitors on cruises around the Solent and Southampton Water. Three generations after James Percy, his grandson Michael is a director with his son Andrew, together with a nephew, Peter Walker, they carry on the family tradition.

Railway tracks had been laid along the pier in 1909 for hand propelled trolleys to carry goods and luggage, but in 1922 this was replaced by the electric railway which was able to take passengers to and from the ferry, a great improvement for everyone using it ever since. The electricity required was

Hythe pier head in the 1920s. The Royal Motor Yacht Club's premises with their pennant flying.

generated near the pier office and part of the village was also supplied for the first time.

The pier had other uses besides getting to and from the ferry. It was a convenient place for anglers to fish away from the shore, as well as for yachtsmen to moor their boats. In 1894 a clubhouse for the Hythe Sailing Club was built at the seaward end attracting many fine yachts to the moorings. The club vacated it in 1914, and afterwards in 1921, it was refurbished to be the headquarters of the Royal Motor Yacht Club and in the next racing season they announced the existence of, "...comfortable and roomy quarters...a large dining room, galley, bar and four sleeping cabins...besides a bathroom". Michael Percy says that they also had a wine cellar below the pier decking reached by a trapdoor!

Miss Kingham, daughter of the builder who put the first railway track along the pier, talked to us at length about her girlhood days. An articulate 80 year-old she remembered Hythe before the first World War when, "There were Royal yachts off-shore and so many other large ones. Sir Thomas Lipton's and Marconi's *Electra* among them".

Many famous people landed from the yachts, Princess Henry of Battenburg was a frequent visitor and Miss Kingham may have been in the group of excited children who greeted the King of Spain and his entourage as they came ashore in 1906 en route for Beaulieu and Highcliffe Castle. She was quite indignant as she remembered an incident on a Hospital Sunday when with, "...the children all in fancy dress, the procession was scattered as the Kaiser in his car swept along the route!"

From the day of its opening, the pier has been a promenade from which to view the shipping of Southampton, large ocean going vessels and small sailing craft alike. Even today, when the *QE2* or the *Canberra* are due to arrive or depart the pier is thronged with onlookers.

Many of those using the ferry in the years between the wars were employees of new industries which flourished in Hythe. Perhaps this is the place to look at the story of the man who became known as 'The Red Fox of Hythe'.

Hubert Scott-Paine, 'Scotty' to his close friends, was certainly one of the most colourful characters in the story of Hythe. A gifted visionary without doubt, forceful, dogmatic, stubborn to some and positively obstinate to others; kind, thoughtful, generous and caring to many more. He was the Waterside's largest employer in the thirties and during the Second World War when more than 1500 men and women were working here to build fleets of small boats to serve the Navy and the R.A.F. in many different roles.

He never lived in Hythe and his work here was but a part of his life; to appreciate his achievements properly you must read Adrian Rance's book *Fast Boats and Flying Boats*, for Scotty came here only when he had sold his Supermarine Company, left his flying days behind him in 1927 and purchased the Hythe shipyard. As a member of the Royal Motor Yacht Club, he had been involved with fast motor boats for some while. The Club at Hythe hosted the 1920 British International Motor Boat Trophy contest for the Harmsworth Trophy which was won by

Shipyard workers at Hythe, perhaps the May, Harden and May Company in Shore Road, before 1914.

A Hythe boatyard in 1912, The Slips, at this time the firm was Stevens, later R. Kemp & Co.

A 35' luxury speed boat from Scott-Paine's Power Boat Company in the 1930s.

Scott-Paine's Miss Britain III which took the world water speed record in 1933 at an average of 100.132 mph.

the American, Garfield Wood, the legendary Grey Fox of Algonac, the fastest man on water for many years. The ambition to beat this man, win this trophy for England and hold the world water speed record was just one of the reasons Scott-Paine bought the Hythe yard. At the same time he foresaw the sport and leisure potential for small fast boats and knew that American firms could flood this market as they had done with popular cars. He lost no time, cleared the site in Shore Road, recruited a design team, coined the name *The British Power Boat Company* and started at once to build small, fast, seaworthy craft.

His designs were new, his ideas and methods well ahead of his time. The factory itself was clean and tidy, craftsmen wore white overalls, were encouraged to take a pride in their work and in the workplace. Incentive schemes for apprenticeship, welfare facilities and mobile canteens were introduced. A succession of craft, graded in size, performance and degree of luxury went down the slipways and sold readily. Their owners enjoyed many of the facilities common in today's marinas, more than half a century later. Winter lay-up, fuel and stores, maintenance by specialised mechanics, car parks, rest rooms, a club house, were all available at Hythe and were widely advertised.

In 1929, in a closely guarded workshop, a challenge for the World Championship had been built in secret. Henry Seagrave, who had taken the world land speed record at Daytona Beach in his *Golden Arrow*, now raced Scotty's boat *Miss England* against 'Gar' Wood's *Miss America VII* and won the Harmsworth Trophy, but not the world water speed record. The next year Scott-Paine took his *Miss Britain I* to America, brought back the Detroit News Trophy, and defended it at Hythe in 1931. His later boats, *Miss Britain II* and *Miss Britain III* won many international events, culminating in the gaining of the World Water Speed record in Southampton Water in 1933. *Miss Britain III* was the first boat ever to travel on sea water at more than 100 mph and for several years was the fastest single-engined boat in the world.

Before this, Scott-Paine's vision for Britain had been of a 'Mile-a-Minute Navy' and he spent years trying to persuade the authorities to invest in small, light, very fast warships; it was to be a long, slow, frustrating task. His civilian designs were the basis for these ideas and in 1931 the Air Ministry bought a prototype which was delivered to R.A.F. Mount Batten, Plymouth where service trials were carried out by Aircraftman Shaw. Lawrence shared Scotty's views on small, fast, easily manoeuvrable warships

and was seconded to Hythe to test the installation of new engines in the boat which became the R.A.F. 200 class.

Writing to Lady Astor In March 1931 Lawrence said,

> ...Tomorrow I get a change from Mount Batten, as I go to Hythe, near Southampton, for ten days instruction in a new fast motor boat being built for the R.A.F. Not very fast, I'm afraid, but faster than the old crocks.

He lodged at Myrtle Cottage in St John's Street with Mrs Biddlecombe whose husband had been Scotty's steward on his yacht. (It is now unnamed, but is the last house on the left of the road, since used as offices and next to the old factory site. It is not the house in South Street nearby with the same name).

The following August virtually the whole of the works was destroyed by fire and Scott-Paine had to start all over again. The site was cleared immediately by the staff with local people pressed in to help. The new buildings, with new plant, equipment and even more up to date methods, quickly became, "The most efficient motor boat factory in the world".

The R.A.F.200 class boats were delivered on time and Lawrence wrote from Myrtle Cottage in June 1932 to Col. Newcombe,

A 37'6" armoured target boat at Hythe in 1932 for Air Ministry inspection.

...I base here, and test or tune motor boats for a living. A poor living – 3/9d (19p) a day – but interesting and I get what I want done. Our boats would interest you. One goes to Malta in August...

In the thirties Scott-Paine, besides his pleasure craft, developed many different sizes of boats for various uses, gun boats, torpedo boats, seaplane tenders, armoured target launches, admiralty barges and picket boats amongst them. They were employed in many countries and when war came Scott-Paine was in America negotiating for the purchase of suitable engines and to try to set up an alternative factory in case Hythe should be destroyed by enemy action. He stayed on to organise the licensing of his designs in the U.S.A. and a new plant in Canada to supply boats for other theatres of war.

Marchwood House (now Marchwood Priory) was bought and became a residential training centre. Later on, workshops set up there helped the Hythe works to continue, despite severe difficulties including bomb damage. Here and at the war-time plant at Poole, they built many hundreds of boats for the Navy and the Air Force. Many airmen, forced to ditch in the Channel and elsewhere owed their lives to the Air Sea Rescue 68 foot High Speed Launches, familiarly known to the R.A.F. as 'Hants and Dorsets'.

After the war there were few orders for boats, but it was hoped to replace them with the mass-production of timber pre-fabricated houses under the *Scottwood* name. The prototype was eventually erected at Hythe Hospital. Sufficient timber however could not be allocated for this by the government and the yard was closed in 1946. Scott-Paine died in America in 1954; his factory has been put to different uses since then, the manufacture of surgical plasters and electric blankets among them. At the time of writing the buildings await demolition. It is an eerie experience indeed to stand in the empty spaces, climb dark stairways and imagine the factory filled with people, machinery, boats, the bustle of work and to sense the spirit of its creator.

Yankee Clipper off Hythe in June 1939 with the first direct mails from New York, non-stop.

Using the ferry in those pre-war days, one could not miss seeing the latest form of travel, the graceful Empire flying boats moored off Hythe. The sight of one of these taking off bound for Africa or India and beyond was a sight to remember.

South of the old ship yard that Scott-Paine had bought was reclaimed land and on it were the long hangars which now house the United States base and its marine craft. These sheds had been built by the Admiralty during the first World War for the construction of flying boats. The boat builders, May, Harden and May were well able to do this as the hulls were in effect small boats, and some 80 Felixstowe aircraft were completed there. After the war and about the same time that Scott-Paine bought the shipyard, the sheds were taken over by Vickers Supermarine. When the Empire Air Mail Scheme was set up in 1934 to enable letters to be sent anywhere in the Empire without surcharge, Imperial Airways chose Southampton as the centre for this service. They bought 28 new C-Class Empire flying boats and the Vickers sheds at Hythe became their maintenance base. In 1937 *Caledonia* made the first proving flight across the Atlantic from Hythe to Botwood in Newfoundland via Foynes on the River Shannon. The Empire's air routes were extended to many other countries in the years before the war. To begin with passengers arriving at Southampton docks by train were ferried in comfortable launches (built by the British Power Boat Company) to flying boats docked between twin pontoons just off Hythe, but this facility was later moved to the docks themselves.

Attempts to cross the Atlantic non-stop were made in the thirties and during air-refuelling experiments *Connemara* was burnt out at Hythe. More successful for mail flights was the 1938 innovation which involved the *Mayo Composite* aircraft which was *Maia*, a flying boat, lifting *Mercury*, a large seaplane with the fuel capacity needed, to the required cruising altitude.

The Americans however were the first to start a regular direct transatlantic air-mail service and *Yankee Clipper* touched down at Hythe on June 28th, 1939 with letters from New York.

The Hythe maintenance base continued to work on flying boats during the war. Afterwards nearly 900 people were employed there by B.O.A.C. until jet airliners forced the closure of their flying boat services in 1950.

In the spring of 1989, the last airworthy Sunderland flying boat flew into Southampton Water and was moored off Hythe pier. It was *Excalibur VIII*,

The B.O.A.C. base at Hythe, after the Second World War.

formerly *Islander*, converted from a Sunderland Mark III built in 1944 which had served with R.A.F. 201 Squadron, a nostalgic link with times past.

A link with the ferry for 200 years and four generations, the Banks family recorded their memories for Hythe Historians, Susan and her brothers Harry and Arthur remembered their childhood at Prospect Place, Hythe in the early 1900s,

> Father (Henry Banks) was Captain of the ferry and worked on it for 50 years until just before he died at 87. When he started, he used to row people over in a rowing boat...All the big houses had a yacht...men used to work on the yachts in Summer and fish in the winter...we spent a lot of time out on boats, going out fishing, picking up cockles and getting boatloads of firewood.
>
> The times were happier, all the kids made their own fun...games were played on the road, hopscotch, hoops, dibs, marbles, conkers and stilts.

By this time the Drummonds had sold much of their land in and around Hythe for housing. The name Hillyfields and the older buildings in Drummond Road and Alexandra Roads date from this period, while Victoria Road, an extension of School Lane was later made a part of it and became School Road.

The schools themselves also date from about this time although an earlier one existed from around 1812 in a former non-conformist chapel where the Hythe Social Club is now. The headmaster's house and the infants school were opened in 1895, and the juniors moved into the next door building four years later. When the Banks children went there they had to play football in the gravel playground as there were no playing fields. The number of pupils from the Hythe of today is far larger and at present temporary classrooms have to be used to accommodate them.

Below the schools on the opposite side of School Road is the coastguard station, an imposing group of brick houses of 1880 with the royal initials (for Victoria Regina) in stone and from the library car park you can see a fouled anchor similarly set in the rear gable. On the front too can be seen three 'rattlers' on the upper sashes of the bedroom windows. These had a cord attached so that the coastguards could be called out at night without disturbing the neighbourhood. There was accommodation for a bosun, two other men and their families. Before that time the crew of the coastguard

The present St Johns Church (1874), with the earlier (1823) chapel still standing.

boat lodged in the village. In the 1790s there had been a local Riding Officer, a Mr Roe. According to records he was given a grant of land as salary and was described as an agricultural labourer!

For centuries Hythe was part of the ecclesiastical Parish of Fawley and did not have its own church until 1823 when a chapel built with money raised by subscription, was dedicated to St John. The curacy was the gift of the Rector of Fawley. When a separate parish was created, the present St John's church was consecrated nearby in 1874, a much larger building incorporating some of the memorials from the small, earlier chapel.

Many large houses and their gardens were built in the environs of Hythe during Victorian times but only a few have survived. One of the largest was Langdown House, built for George Tate in 1797 and inherited in 1822 by his daughter. In 1849 the Hobart family bought the house and surrounding park which remained in their hands for more than a century. The family produced two Members of Parliament, Sir Joseph Hobart, the only Liberal M.P. sent to Westminster by the New Forest constituency; and best known locally, Sir Robert Henry Hobart Bt. (1836-1928). Older Hythe residents have clear memories of the gentleman, who lined up his staff on the drive in front of the house to issue his instructions for their day's duties. In the 1920's the Hobarts vigorously opposed the building of the Totton to Fawley railway. They said it would be clearly visible from the house and the embankment would obstruct their view of the shoreline. Earlier attempts to plan the line had been unsuccessful but agreement was reached this time by skirting the Hobart grounds and the first passenger train arrived in Hythe Station in 1925. Miss Irene Hobart who later lived in Dibden Purlieu was a talented artist and her watercolours give us glimpses of Hythe village and its surroundings of a century ago.

In the 1930s Langdown House was used by B.O.A.C. and in the last war it became the ward room of H.M.S. Diligence, a naval base on the Shore Road at Hythe. By 1961 the park land had already been sold to the District Council for housing and the house was sold at auction that year for re-development. The Tate and Hobart families are remembered in the names of roads in what is now Langdown Estate.

Knightons, where the Waitrose complex now stands, was a large house whose high, black, garden wall dominated the end of Hythe High Street. Charles Kelsall bought the house in 1839 and called it the Villa Amalthaea, enlarging it and constructing a sea wall behind which he placed a row of busts of his favourite heroes. Another owner was Capt. Phillips Cosby Lovett who bought it as a waterside home and kept his schooner *Constance* moored beyond the sea wall. He had a Spanish crew and used to disappear for long spells to unknown places.

Later owners of Knightons like those of many of the big houses in and around Hythe, allowed their gardens to be used for fêtes, garden parties and other events, especially when money was needed for charity. In 1919, the idea for a much-needed cottage hospital as a memorial to those local men who had fallen in the War, took shape. Col. Vere Hobart offered land between South Street and New Road for the building, but the total of all the amounts contributed, large and small, fell short of the target. A committee of local landowners, tradespeople and others, chaired by Mrs Vere Hobart decided to buy a house in Atheling Road and adapt it for the purpose. Col. and Mrs Hobart were living in Westcliffe Hall which had been a wartime hospital like Cadland House and they were able to donate many of the supplies needed. The Hospital was opened in 1922 and dedicated by the Bishop of Southampton.

Fund raising continued with the intention of building an entirely new hospital, but in 1939 it was realised that the need was imperative. The White House was bought from Mr Barlow and the move from Atheling Road was made in 1940. This house had formerly been owned by Sir Henry Ewart who had been equerry to Queen Victoria and whose name is perpetuated in the Ewart Recreation Ground.

The hospital, on the Beaulieu Road to Dibden Purlieu and now surrounded by housing, with its Medical Centre and Ambulance Station, still serves the Waterside well. Hythe Hospital fête continues to raise funds for its additional needs and one of those fund raising events of the 30s, 'Football on the Mud' was revived after the last war, again for charity, but had to be moved to a fresh muddy patch when the original 'ground' was reclaimed. It has now been joined by a raft race and a bed push to raise large sums annually for local charities.

On the crest of the next hill towards Dibden Purlieu, Windmill Copse is on the site of another estate. Here was Windmill House, the home of Sir Frederick Stanley Hewitt who was medical adviser to the Royal family in the thirties. The house took its name from the windmill itself, which must have been an imposing tower, to judge from the sketch made by Southampton artist Frederick Lee Bridell which is now in Southampton Art Gallery. When new houses were being built the circular foundations

Langdown House, 1892, a watercolour by Miss I.M. Hobart.

Windmill near Hythe, sketch by F. Lee Bridell.

Westcliffe Hall, home of Col. Vere Hobart, a 1914-1918 hospital and later, Westcliffe Hall Hotel.

A composite view card of Dibden Purlieu from the 1940s.

came to light and were photographed in case they should be destroyed, but they were happily incorporated into one of the gardens as a feature.

We are now in Dibden Purlieu itself in the ecclesiastical parish of Dibden, very near to the boundary of The New Forest. The word Purlieu itself means, "The land that once was afforested".

However the road to Beaulieu is now a busy shopping centre and gone forever are most of the copses and wooded valleys which were the haunt of wildlife and the secret hiding places in tangled undergrowth from where the nightingales of Dibden Purlieu sang in springtime. Not so many years ago we visited a wooded dell in the garden of a large house off Mullins Lane to watch from a hide, a family of badgers feeding and playing. Soon afterwards houses were built over the valley, but the badgers had been safely transferred to a new home in the Forest.

Beaulieu Road before the shopping centre.

Chapter Seven

Dibden to Marchwood and Eling

Dibden is described as Depedene in the Domesday Survey, the name meaning a dell of thick wood (Anglo-Saxon Deop, *deep* and Den, *a wooded valley or dell*. It possessed a saltern and a fishery.

The church of All Saints, Dibden, is of uncertain age though its list of Rectors starts with Master Ralph in 1262 and the Chancel Arch is of 13th Century style. It was the first church in Britain to be damaged in the Second World War, when in July 1940 incendiary bombs set it, and the Dibden Manor house alongside, alight. Much was lost; Communion rails of yew with twisted baluster shafts dating from 1660; 14th Century stained glass in the Chancel and the 13th Century font was damaged when the bells crashed down from the tower.

Restoration in 1955 included the demolition of the north aisle and the lowering of the south aisle walls to enclose a Garden of Remembrance while the rubble stone was used to build the new walls to

Hollybank Lodge on the road to Dibden.

All Saints Church, Dibden, as it was before the war.

July 1940 – The morning after the bombs fell.

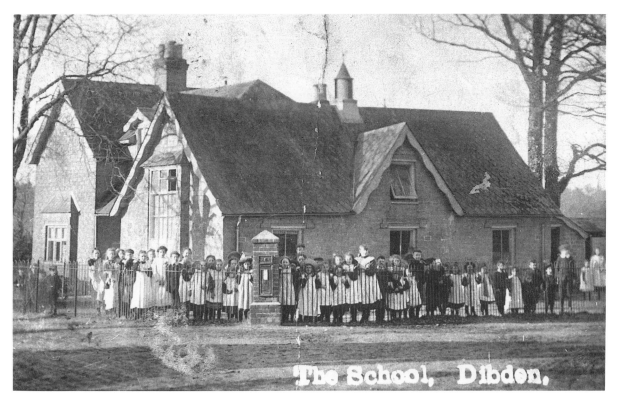

Dibden school, an early postcard from about 1900.

the nave. Two bells were cast from the metal salvaged from the tower and the font was repaired. At the same time the floor was lowered to its original level and the church is now much simpler but of great beauty.

Under the Chancel is the vault of the Lisle family of Moyles Court who were associated with the ownership of the Manor of Dibden by marriage and in the churchyard are other memorials to them as well as to the Wyatt family. One tombstone of Joseph Wyatt of 1757 has carved busts of husband and wife, with a heart above, a ship and their four children. The Wyatts owned land throughout the Waterside including, "a house called Racketts at Hythe" and supplied timber for Janverin's shipbuilding at Hamble and Lepe.

The marshy banks of Southampton Water in Dibden Bay and northwards to Eling were unsuited for shipbuilding. Towards the end of the 18th Century, Lord Malmesbury owned the Manor of Dibden and improved the shore by financing the building of a sloping breakwater wall by Thomas King of Eling.

Beyond Dibden is the village of Marchwood; in Domesday it was recorded as Mercewode and held by the King. Marchwood has access to the water at Cracknore Hard and like Hythe, this was a short

ferry passage to Southampton. Horace Barkham was born at the *Ship Inn* on the Hard itself in 1917 and remembered his father running the ferry service to and from the opposite shore. Later he had a small fleet of motor boats offering trips around the docks to view the big ships. When his father died in 1935, he took over the business and developed it from Southampton as *Blue Funnel Cruises*.

A row of white cottages in the heart of the village was bought in 1910 by Edward Gooding from Henry Lloyd of Byams House and when these were restored by the Hampshire Buildings Preservation Trust in the 1970s, the original structure was found to have been a single large barn. Kelly's Directory of 1891 recorded that the owner, William Gascoigne JP, was then in residence at Byams House. This had been rebuilt in 1878, the family having lived there for over a century. The *New Forest Magazine* of August 1913 tells of a School Treat in July.

The children attending the schools were entertained in a most generous way by Major and Mrs Lloyd at Byams. The weather was fine and pleasant and everything was provided by our host and hostess to give the children a real good time. Roundabouts, swings, coconut shies

A cottage in Dibden.

Marchwood Park, private house, a war-time boat 'factory', then a school, now a private hospital.

Sansom's shop at Marchwood.

Near Marchwood Church, the post mark is 1905.

Cracknore Hard Marchwood, in front of the Ship Inn, 1920s.

The Ship Inn, at present the offices of Husbands Shipyards Ltd.

cricket, were all in their turn enjoyed by big and little. An excellent tea was partaken of by about 140 children. Before dispersing at 8.30 hearty thanks corroborated by enthusiastic cheers were tendered to Major Lloyd and family for giving us a thoroughly enjoyable afternoon and evening.

Byams House is now the Officers' Mess for the Military Port.

Magazine Lane, Marchwood, got its name in 1815 when the Government Powder Magazine was opened to store vast quantities of gunpowder for the forces. There were three magazines, various handling rooms, barracks, a pier, a canal and a landing hard. The Admiralty took it over in 1891 as the Royal Naval Armament Depot and used it to its full capacity, prompting a petition from Southampton for its removal in view of the danger to the town. It suffered a devastating air attack in June 1940 when incendiary bombs destroyed vast quantities of ammunition and cordite, fortunately without injury to any one although the heat was intense. The Officer in Charge, Mr H.D. Robbins and Police Sergeant Goodyear were both awarded the George Medal and two other policemen received British Empire Medals for their conduct.

The *Ship Inn* is now the offices of Husbands Shipyard, a family firm started when Mr J.B. Husband came here in 1924 with his six sons and seven daughters. Building and repairing yachts gave way to wartime invasion barges and motor minesweepers which were launched here and towed to Beaulieu river for fitting out. After the war commercial ship repairs, particularly of tankers took over and now the founder's sons and four of his grandsons control a wide-ranging engineering business with ship repairing (container vessels, ferries etc), industrial, electrical and heating divisions. As part of redevelopment it is planned to restore the *Ship Inn* to its former use.

The land on which Marchwood Military Port is situated was partly reclaimed in the thirties from mud flats and taken over by the government in 1943. Large elements of the prefabricated Mulberry harbours were built and launched here for the Normandy landings. It is now the home of 17 Port & Maritime Regiment, Royal Corps of Transport and has been greatly extended and updated to provide a road, rail, and sea facility for moving the

Byams House Marchwood, owned by the Lloyd family at the beginning of the century, now the Officers' Mess of Marchwood Military Port.

armed forces quickly and efficiently. At the time of the Falklands conflict its role in handling the support ships was crucial and the loss of *L.S.L.* (Landing Ship, Logistic) *Sir Galahad* was a severe blow to the port.

Those men of R.C.T. Marchwood who died in that short, fierce war, are remembered in a memorial and small garden by Marchwood Parish Church, with the badges of the ships and a representation of one of them on a slate slab set in a large boulder from the Islands. The Corps has again taken an important part recently in the Gulf war.

Very near to Marchwood is Eling village, its church, dedicated to St Mary is on the crown of a steep hill with water on three sides, a good strategic position easily defended in ancient times. This may well have been the site of a Saxon settlement although the name derives from Edlinges, a word of even earlier Celtic origin. A wooden church was probably built here after St Birinus came to the area in the sixth century, but the present building dates from about 1050. Portions of the fabric are certainly very early Norman work and Domesday records that in the manor of Edlinges which was held by the King, "… there is a church here with half a carucate of land belonging to it in charity…" A carucate was about 100 acres, so it was obviously a valuable property and an important place, the village itself was larger than nearby Totton with three hundred villagers, mills, saltings and a fishery as well as the church.

This beautiful building, like the other Waterside churches, was greatly altered and extended in the 13th, 14th and 15th centuries and at the Reformation the Manor of Eling was granted to Lord Sandys, Lord Chamberlain and Constable of Southampton. His family is believed to have given the church its prized possession, a painting of the Last Supper which is probably of the Venetian school, perhaps by Bonifazio (1487-1553) or his assistants. Early this century it was placed behind the altar in a panelled wall to be more easily seen.

Many memorials have survived in the church and there are some very interesting gravestones in the churchyard which extends down the hill on the northern side. Genealogists should buy, besides the brief guide to St Mary's, the "Extracts from Church Records" by Thomas Thistle, a former vicar, republished by the Totton and Eling Historical Society. It contains hundreds of names from the registers which are among the oldest in Hampshire, dating from 1537. The photograph was kindly made available to us by the Society and their records show that it was taken about 1860 by Anne Crooke of the 'Village Bells'. There was at that time a group of narrow cottages between the church and the road. Looking at the site now it hardly seems to have been possible. The gentleman in the tall stove pipe hat was James Callan, grandfather of Frank Mayor.

The hill from the church runs steeply down to a very old causeway across the Bartley Water and at least one of the mills mentioned in Domesday may have used tidal power, for here is the only working Tidal Mill in the world, described in an excellent book, "The Tide Mill at Eling" and we must leave you to read it and visit the mill to wonder at it, for our circuit of the Waterside Parishes must end here at the water's edge.

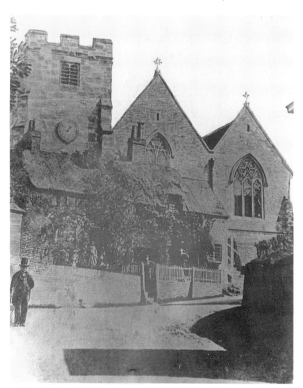

Eling Church about 1860.

Bibliography

Eaglehurst and Luttrell's Folly. Brian Buxton (Privately produced)

Seaplanes and Flying Boats of the Solent. Ed. Adrian Rance (Southampton University Industrial Archaeology Group. 1981)

Fast Boats and Flying Boats. Adrian Rance (Ensign Publications. 1989)

The New Forest, Its History and Scenery. J.R. Wise (1883, republished S.R. Publishers. 1971)

The Drummonds of Charing Cross. H. Bolitho and D. Peel (Allen and Unwin. 1967)

The Schneider Trophy Contest, 50th Anniversary. Ed. D. Molton (Schneider 81. 1981)

The Calshot and Fawley Narrow Gauge Railways. F.W. Cooper (Plateway Press. 1989)

Lively Ahoy! G.W. Bowyer (Dedicated to the Trinity House Pilots. 1930)

Henry VIII and the Development of Coastal Defence. (H.M.S.O. 1976)

Calshot Castle. J.G. Coad (Historic Buildings and Monuments Commission. 1986)

The Tide Mill at Eling. Diana Smith (Ensign Publications. 1989)

The Solent Sky. Peter T. New (Southampton Printers. 1976)

Hythe Pier and Ferry – A History. Alan Titheridge (Itchen Printers. 1981)

My Father Marconi. Degna Marconi (Frederick Muller Ltd. 1962)

The Letters of T.E. Lawrence. David Garnett (Jonathan Cape. 1938)

Springboard for Overlord. Anthony Kemp (Milestone Publications. 1984)

A Solent Flight. Ivor J. Hilliker (Kingfisher Publications. 1990)

Our Exbury. A.J. Holland and Edmund de Rothschild (Paul Cave. 1982)

A Wild Heritage. The History and Nature of the New Forest. Terry Heathcote (Ensign Publications. 1990)

St. Mary's Eling – A church guide

Extracts from Church Records. T. Thistle (Totton & Eling Historical Society)

Acknowledgements

Besides those anonymous helpers already mentioned in the preface we would like to thank the many other individuals and organisations who have assisted us in various ways to produce this book. We hope we have not omitted anyone from this list of names, but apologise in advance if indeed we have. Thanks therefore to: D.C.Abbott, F.Alexander, E.Anderson, H.S.Banks, R.E.F.Barker, F.Baker, H.W.Bailey, G.L.Blay, British Airways (B.O.A.C.), B.Buxton, W.Hopwood, G.S.Bowen, C.Bowyer, B.R.Burnett, K.Child, A.Coat, J.Cockoram, A.B.Codd, F.Cole, A.Corbishey, F.W.Cooper, S.E.Cooper, A.F.Drewitt, M.Drummond, D.M.Eley, English Heritage, Esso Petroleum Co. Ltd, J.Fairman, *Hampshire Magazine*, William Heinemann Ltd, V.Hodgkinson, A.J.Holland, Husbands, Marchwood, D.Jary, K.Martin, F.Mayo, Revd. C.R.Miles, D.Moldon, E.Mosenthal, E.& B.Mudge, G.Parkes, M.Percy, G.Petty, A.Rance, E.de Rothschild, T.Soffe, P.Somes, G.South, Southampton City Art Gallery, G.Southern, P.Talbot, A.Titheridge, *Waterside Observer*, Totton and Eling Historical Society, M.Wills, P.Whittington, P. Wilson, R.Woolhead, 3 Transport Group R.C.T., Marchwood.

The illustrations are all reproduced from photographs in the Fawley Historians' collection excepting the following: Pages 18, 22, 43, 49, from a private collection. Pages 10, 17, 18, 19, 39, 50, 52, by kind permission of Mr Maldwin Drummond.

Index

SURNAMES

SHIPS, YACHTS, FERRY BOATS & BARGES

FARMS